D0631172

Napoleon
and Europe

D.G. Wright

An imprint of **Pearson Education**

Harlow, England · London · New York · Reading, Massachusetts · San Francisco
Toronto · Don Mills, Ontario · Sydney · Tokyo · Singapore · Hong Kong · Seoul
Taipei · Cape Town · Madrid · Mexico City · Amsterdam · Munich · Paris · Milan

Pearson Education Limited
Edinburgh Gate, Harlow
Essex CM20 2JE, England
and Associated Companies throughout the world.

Visit us on the World Wide Web at:
http://www.pearsoned.co.uk

First published 1984

Set in 10/11pt Linotron Baskerville
Printed in Malaysia, PP
ISBN 0-582-35457-9

British Library Cataloguing in Publication Data

Wright, D.G.
  Napoleon and Europe.—(Seminar· studies
  in history)
  1. Napoléon I, *Emperor of the French*
  I. Title   II. Series
  944.05'092'4   DC203

  ISBN 0-582-35457-9

Library of Congress Cataloging in Publication Data

Wright, D.G.
  Napoleon and Europe.
  (Seminar studies in history)
  Bibliography: p.
  Includes index.
  1. Napoleon I, Emperor of the French, 1769–1821.
  2. France—History—1789–1815. 3. Europe—History—1789–1815.
  I. Title. II. Series.
  DC203.W87   1984   940.2'7'0924   84–756
  ISBN 0-582-35457-9 (pbk.)

18 17
05 04 03

Contents

Contents

For Valerie and Timothy

Acknowledgements

I am pleased to record my gratitude to Roger Lockyer for his generous advice, to Clive Emsley of the Open University for helpful suggestions, and to my daughter Victoria for both encouragement and criticism.

The Publishers are grateful to Macmillan Publishing Co. Inc. and Librairie Plon for permission to reproduce an extract from H. Miles' translation of *Memoirs of General le Caulincourt* edited by J. Hanoteau.

Seminar Studies in History

Introduction

The Seminar Studies series was conceived by Patrick Richardson, whose experience of teaching history persuaded him of the need for something more substantial than a textbook chapter but less formidable than the specialised full-length academic work. He was also convinced that such studies, although limited in length, should provide an up-to-date and authoritative introduction to the topic under discussion as well as a selection of relevant documents and a comprehensive bibliography.

Patrick Richardson died in 1979, but by that time the Seminar Studies series was firmly established, and it continues to fulfil the rôle he intended for it. This book, like others in the series, is therefore a living tribute to a gifted and original teacher.

Note on the System of References:
A bold number in round brackets (**5**) in the text refers the reader to the corresponding entry in the Bibliography section at the end of the book. A bold number in square brackets, preceded by 'doc' [**doc. 6**] refers the reader to the corresponding items in the section of Documents, which follows the main text.

Part One: Cadet to Consul

1 The Corsican Frenchman

Napoleon's enormous natural talents would have earned him success in any profession at any time. Nevertheless he was lucky to be born at Ajaccio in Corsica in 1769. In the previous year the island of Corsica had been ceded to France by the Republic of Genoa, so that Napoleon was only narrowly born a Frenchman and a subject of Louis XV. For a time his father was involved in resistance to French occupation, but soon changed sides and became prominent in the French administration of his homeland. Although Napoleon's social status was to remain somewhat ambiguous in French eyes, he was clearly of noble lineage in Corsican terms. Not only did his family possess a landed estate, but his father was able to demonstrate to the King's chief herald the documentary proof of nobility necessary to send his son to military academies in France, closed to commoners before 1789. That many Frenchmen regarded Corsican nobility as inferior to their own eventually worked to Napoleon's benefit, since after the outbreak of the Revolution in 1789 he was never placed by fervent Republicans in the hated and vulnerable category of 'former aristocrat'. It is doubtful whether he ever really regarded himself as a Frenchman. Corsican society, with its strong emotional ties of family and friendship and fierce vendettas against enemies, was closer to the clan relationships of the Scottish Highlands than to the culture of France (**31**, Ch. 1). Always fluent in his native Italian, Napoleon learned French as a second language, speaking it with a heavy accent and unable to write it grammatically. His Mediterranean origins enabled him to view France with a certain objectivity, which frequently verged on cynicism. For him it was never *la patrie*.

In 1778 the nine-year-old 'Napoleone' was despatched to the military accademy at Brienne in Champagne, after a three-month intensive French language course at Autun. Living under a Spartan regime and mocked by his fellow pupils for his fierce pride and halting French, he was not to see his parents again for years. At Brienne, more of a preparatory school than a military academy proper, Napoleon received the conventional education of a young gentleman of the time, revealing an unusual ability in history and mathematics, while compensating for his loneliness and lack of the social graces by voracious reading (**38**, Pt i, Ch. 1). In 1784, at the age of fourteen, he was lucky enough to gain free admission as a King's Cadet to the *Ecole Militaire* in Paris, one of the élite institutions of the *ancien régime*. In that year there was a special intake of mathematically-gifted boys destined for the artillery arm. The *Ecole Militaire* offered a first-class general education and here Napoleon was taught by some of the most eminent tutors in France. His sharp mind and remarkable powers of intense application resulted in his passing the highly competitive examination for entry to the artillery officer branch in one year, rather than the usual two or three. He was then commissioned in the *Régiment de la Fère*, one of the most efficient and admired regiments in the royal army. While he was stationed at Valence from 1785 to 1788, Napoleon's theoretical and practical training continued: chemistry, physics, mathematics, engineering-drawing, gunnery, drill and tactics (**29**, Ch. 1).

Officers in the royal army received generous periods of leave, and between 1786 and 1788 Napoleon spent three-quarters of his time either in Paris or his native Corsica. Hence there was ample time to fulfil his self-imposed programme of reading and diligent note-taking in history and literature, as well as in science and professional military studies. The outbreak of the French Revolution occurred while Napoleon's regiment was at Auxonne, although his own active role was confined to suppressing local food riots and quashing a regimental mutiny in July 1789. Like many of his fellow young officers from the lesser nobility, Napoleon approved of the Revolution in principle, while disliking the increasingly frequent disorder and crowd violence. He was strongly influenced by Enlightenment writers like Montesquieu and Rousseau, who argued that institutions like the church, the monarchy and the nobility, as well as the inefficient system of administration and the structure of feudal landownership, could be fundamentally reformed by the application of rational quasi-scientific principles. By such means, the sum of human happiness could be increased and the perfectibility of man realized.

At the same time, however, Napoleon developed a taste not only for the writings of the romantic Rousseau, but also for those seventeenth-century authors like Corneille, whose classic heroes were devoted to their duty and their destiny. Such reading helped to deepen his own dreams of heroic glory (**25**, Vol. i, Ch. 3).

Napoleon therefore welcomed the French Revolution, not only because of the opportunity it provided for putting Enlightenment principles into practice, but also for the possibilities it opened up for talented and ambitious young men like himself to make their mark by means of a combination of energy, will-power and shrewd calculation. Yet Napoleon's enthusiasm for the Revolution was always selective. He cared nothing for the basic principle of popular sovereignty; hierarchy and authority were perfectly acceptable, provided they were founded on 'rational' principles. The young Corsican was neither a democrat nor a humanitarian, as he exhibited the professional soldier's characteristic hostility to crowd violence and 'anarchy'. Undisciplined rioters deserved blowing to pieces. Visiting Paris in August 1792, he witnessed the second attack on the Tuileries by the Paris crowd and was horrified by the sight of market women savagely mutilating the corpses of Swiss Guards. Henceforth he was to harbour an intense fear of the common people of Paris. For him, the Revolution was that of the *philosophes*: not that of the *sans culottes* (**38**, Ch. 3).

During 1790 and 1791 Napoleon was in Corsica, enforcing French rule in the island. By 1792, however, he had tired of this backwater and went to join the French army in Italy. On the way he passed close to Toulon, a major naval base which had rebelled against the Revolutionary regime in Paris and admitted the English and Spanish fleets. When a French army was sent to besiege the city, Napoleon saw his chance for glory and, through the intervention of one of his Corsican patrons, succeeded in gaining command of the artillery section. He then drew up a plan which succeeded brilliantly. After a four-month siege, Napoleon's artillery assumed control of the harbour and forced the enemy fleets to evacuate. It was at Toulon in 1793 that Napoleon first displayed his military genius: his keen eye for tactical possibilities, his skill and confidence in organizing men and supplies, his single-minded pursuit of his objective and his ability to mould an efficient fighting-force from disorganized and ill-disciplined troops (**67**, Pt i). As a reward he was promoted to Brigadier-General at the age of twenty-four, while his exploits attracted the attention of Barras, *représentant en mission* with the army and soon to become one of the most powerful men in France. The fact that Napoleon had written a pro-Jacobin pamphlet and had joined the political circle of Augustin Robespierre, brother of Maximilien, made him ideologically acceptable to the Revolutionary government and led to his appointment as chief planner of the operations of the Army of

Italy, a post which enabled him to reveal his gift for mapping-out grand strategy (**38**, Pt i, Ch. 3).

In the summer of 1794, however, Napoleon narrowly missed the guillotine. When Maximilien Robespierre and his supporters fell during the crisis of Thermidor, their gifted young protégé came under suspicion as a terrorist. He was saved by the fact that he was far away from Paris and that his case was investigated by Saliceti, his old Corsican patron. After only a fortnight's imprisonment in the fortress of Antibes, Napoleon was able to return to his staff work with the Army of Italy, subsequently impressing leading politicians with the feasibility of his plan for an invasion of the Italian peninsula. It was his carefully cultivated contacts with leading politicians that provided him with his next chance to come to public attention in the crisis of Vendémiaire (October) 1795, when he was appointed second-in-command to Barras in charge of the government forces which put down a popular revolt in Paris. Napoleon's notorious 'whiff' of grapeshot' blasted hundreds of rioters with cannon-fire. This time his reward was promotion to Major-General and command of the Army of the Interior. Soon afterwards he married Josephine de Beauharnais, a fashionable and beautiful thirty-two-year-old Creole widow and a former mistress of Barras. Meanwhile there was a new system of government in France. The constitution of 1795 created the Directory, whereby central executive authority was vested in five 'directors', responsible to two legislative bodies, the Council of the Ancients and the Council of Five Hundred, elected by a restricted property-owning franchise. Finding it difficult to attract mass loyalty at home, the new government looked abroad to increase its reputation by an aggressive and expansionary foreign policy.

By now Napoleon was a celebrated figure in French Revolutionary society. None of the other talented and ambitious generals who had also made useful political friendships and had survived the vicissitudes of the end of the Great Terror in 1794 possessed the naked ambition and icy calculation of the young Corsican. At the age of twenty-six he was given command of the Army of Italy, as much for his proven ability and meticulous and imaginative plans for the invasion of Lombardy as for his influential military contacts, political friendships and talent for self-publicity. Nevertheless, the appointment was something of a calculated risk on the part of the new Directorial government, for the young general was untried as an independent field commander. In the event, his success exceeded all expectations.

2 The Art of Warfare

However varied the assessments of Napoleon's career, few historians would deny that he raised the art and science of war to new
heights. That he was able to do so depended to a considerable
extent on the fact that he could draw upon the progress made in
the French royal army of the *ancien régime* and on the fervour of the
Republican armies, representing 'the nation in arms', from 1792.
Hence the stroke of luck in his being born during an age of
substantial military innovation; for a major revolution in warfare in
fact predated Napoleon's accession to power and high command
(**72**, Ch. 4). Clausewitz, himself a participant in the Revolutionary
and Napoleonic wars, provided the classic summary of this warfare
revolution in his *On War*, published in 1832. The essential features
of the revolution lay not so much in changes in weaponry, tactics
or training, but rather in the substitution of wars of peoples for the
traditional dynastic wars of monarchs. War between Revolutionary
France and the Austrians and Prussians from 1792 marked a
transition from the limited conflicts of the earlier eighteenth century – motivated neither by ideology nor by aggressive nationalism
and aiming to gain mere slivers of territory or to bring about a
dynastic reshuffle – to 'people's wars', based on the concept of 'the
nation in arms'. These wars aimed to obliterate not only enemy
forces, but even enemy states themselves [**doc. 1**].

Such a transition was made possible by a substantial increase in
the size of armies, initially in Revolutionary France as a response
to fears of invasion and the cry of *la patrie en danger* in 1792. The
Revolutionary regime had to be defended at all costs against
potential destruction by the European monarchies. Patriotic volun-
teers, anxious not only to defend liberty but also to carry its alleged
benefits to the deprived peoples of Europe, were later supplemen-
ted by mass conscription. French industrial expansion, coupled
with centralized Revolutionary administrative procedures, made
possible the supply and equipping of these larger armies. In 1793
France produced 7,000 cannon and by the end of the following year
she had a million men under arms. With a population of about

twenty-eight millions to recruit from, the French armies owed a good deal of their success to superiority of numbers over the enemy. Napoleon was to boast that he could afford to expend 30,000 men a month on the battlefield. So far as military recruitment was concerned, Napoleon merely continued Carnot's policy of drawing upon the whole population. In practice, however, there was always a wide range of those exempt from military service. Even in the last-ditch crisis of 1812–13 the government was able to recruit effectively only just under fifty per cent of eligible Frenchmen (**72**, Ch. 9). Nonetheless, nearly two million native-born Frenchmen served in the Imperial armies between 1804 and 1815.

Eighteenth-century wars were usually waged with armies of 50–75,000 men. In his Italian campaign of 1796–7 Napoleon commanded only 35,000. However, by the time of the Ulm and Jena campaigns of 1805–6 numbers had risen to 180–190,000. Other nations imitated the French example. Austria put 100,000 into battle at Wagram in 1809. Prussia fielded nearly 150,000 in 1806, while in 1813 she had 300,000 men under arms, equivalent to six per cent of her population. Changes in weaponry and equipment were relatively limited. French artillery experts in the 1770s and 1780s had designed lighter and more effective field-guns, making use of horse artillery and concentrating cannon in separate regiments in order to achieve maximum fire-power (**69**, Ch. 1). After 1796 Napoleon was quick to apply these innovations and gain considerable superiority over his enemies for some years. He also effectively employed heavy cavalry in shock formations, rather like tanks in the Second World War, while the light cavalry was designed to engage in reconnaissance and pursuit of a fleeing enemy, as at Ulm and Jena. Napoleon also developed further the new French infantry tactics which dated from the closing years of the *ancien régime*. Rather than the traditional line-formation – two or three ranks of musketeers firing continuous volleys – there was increasing use by the Revolutionary armies of massed columns, relying on the bayonet rather than the musket, to charge the enemy. Line formation, however, was never abandoned, and Napoleon became adept at the use of 'mixed order': a combination of line and column as circumstances dictated.

It was the French who also pioneered the organization of armies into self-contained independent *corps d'armée* of 15–30,000 men, able to advance simultaneously at some distance from each other along several roads and capable of engaging superior numbers until reinforced by one of the other corps. Such an articulation of forces involved a significant increase in mobility, especially when the French army no longer depended on elongated and carefully prepared supply trains and magazines. The French Republican armies had been split into several divisions, each capable of 'living off the land' by means of organized requisitioning rather than random plunder. Such a system had the advantage of increased mobility, as well as easing pressure on the over-strained French war economy (**99**, Ch. 3). Yet by the late 1790s this system had degenerated into the undisciplined pillage and plunder of the early and mid-eighteenth century, as the size of armies made it impossible to ensure supplies through organized requisitioning or magazines. This system of existing by plunder was to prove extremely effective in creating a highly mobile army in Italy in 1796–7 and in central Europe later. But its limitations were to be cruelly exposed in the barren wastes of Poland and Russia in 1812 (**55**, Ch. 2).

Napoleon was not a major military reformer, since he operated with the weapons and tactics developed in France when he was a young cadet (**73**, Ch. 1). Many of his favourite manoeuvres, for example his use of the 'central position', were borrowed directly from Frederick the Great. Only from 1805 did he perfect the mass artillery barrage which made him even more feared and celebrated. On the other hand, he was a master of his profession, thoroughly educated in the latest techniques and with the intelligence to apply them flexibly on the battlefield. At the same time, he was careful to continue the Revolutionary tradition of careers open to talent and promotion by merit for bravery in battle. The careers of four of his marshals demonstrate how it was possible to rise from the lowest ranks to the highest in the Revolutionary armies. Although Napoleon introduced various élite corps and special decorations — especially the rather pampered Imperial Guard — these were all open to merit and perhaps helped to boost the morale of the army as a whole. As a skilled propagandist, he was adept at artfully exploiting the revolutionary fervour and *élan* of his troops, as well as their desire for booty and women, even if he reduced army medical services to save money (**25**, Vol. i, Ch. 8). After 1799 he also had the advantage of being the civil as well as the military chief, not answerable to any ruler or government back in his capital.

There is little doubt that it was Napoleon's own political and military genius which enabled the Republican armies, created by Carnot, to score such resounding successes after 1796. Napoleon was a kind of one-man version of the celebrated Prussian General

Staff of the later nineteenth century, able to carry countless details in his head and plan carefully months in advance [**doc. 2**]. He also possessed an uncanny ability to visualize a battle as a whole and to move very large armies, often of more than 200,000 men, over enormous tracts of the European continent at unprecedented speeds. In 1805 he quartered his various army corps, each of about 20,000 men, all over western Europe, but brought them together with meticulous timing to encircle the hapless Austrians at Ulm, before dispersing them again prior to converging rapidly on the Austrians and Russians at Austerlitz. In the following year, the process was repeated against the Prussians (**71**, Ch. 5).

Napoleon's extraordinary facility for calculating precisely how long it would take marching columns of men to rendezvous at a pre-selected point gave him a clear advantage over most of his opponents before 1808. So did his ability to manoeuvre large armies from column to line formation in advantageous positions from which numerically superior forces could be attacked and defeated separately. Napoleonic tactics, involving flanking assaults on the enemy rear and lines of communication, were designed to produce a decisive superiority of both manpower and fire-power at the critical area of the battlefield. No commander was more skilled in detecting the weak spot in the enemy's deployment and then swiftly concentrating his own forces upon it. In his ability to transform warfare into a continuous process, fusing together the march to the battlefield, the actual conflict between armies and the pursuit and destruction of the defeated enemy, Napoleon was unrivalled. No defensive campaign was planned before 1814. Nor did he rely unduly on the lash or the soul-destroying discipline of the old dynastic armies, with their consequent high rate of desertion. His lightning offensive warfare depended more on inspiring his men by skilful propaganda and the promise of glory, promotion and loot [**doc. 3**].

Napoleon's system of rapid mobile warfare dazzled and intimidated European rulers and commanders for some years. But it contained potential weaknesses. Firstly, it depended upon a high degree of personal control by Napoleon himself (**68**, Ch. 6). This was to prove less practicable after 1806 when distances in east Europe and Russia proved too vast. The *Grande Armée* of 1812, with its 600,000 or so men, was simply too large to be controlled efficiently by the Emperor's centralized and personalized chain of command. His method of dictating both strategy and tactics, often down to the last detail, and of failing to develop any kind of autonomous staff organization, deprived his marshals and generals of any opportunity to gain experience of independent command [**doc. 2**]. When Napoleon's marshals were on their own, without the reassuring presence of the Emperor – as in Spain from 1809 – they tended to sink to the level of mediocrity, with the partial exception of Davout and Masséna. Thus enemy commanders learned eventually to avoid armies directly commanded by Napoleon himself, and concentrate on those led by his marshals, as in the Leipzig campaign of 1813.

Secondly, Napoleonic warfare depended upon a constant flow of trained conscripts, but this began to dry up after 1806. Henceforth the quality of recruits deteriorated, while the constant campaigning meant that very little time could be devoted to training them in marching and rapid manoeuvring. Such an army, increasingly reliant on troops from the allied and vassal states, and deprived of the masses of highly-trained cavalry essential for the lightning-strike approach, was suitable only for the prolonged slogging-matches which Napoleon's battles tended to become between 1807 and 1813 (**71**, Ch. 5). Finally, Napoleon's foes learned to imitate his methods, as they too developed mobile tactics and mixed columns, kept their supply-trains closer behind their armies, and introduced massed artillery batteries and flexible cavalry tactics. Above all, they learned to pin down Napoleon in battles of attrition, where their combined superior manpower would eventually prove too much for French *élan* (**67**, Pt iii; **200, 201**).

3 Italy and Egypt

The Republican armies had been created in order to defend France against the forces of the counter-revolutionary monarchies. By 1794 the Republic was safe, yet the Revolutionary government was unwilling to disband its large armies and risk plunging France into further chaos. Nor, after 1795, could the Directory, with its rickety administration and finances, cope with the strain and expense of armies subsisting on French territory (**54**, Ch. 1). The armies had therefore to be pushed outside France, even beyond the 'natural frontiers' of the Alps, Rhine and Pyrenees. Any consequent booty and military glory would then help shore up the Directorial regime, crippled by its lack of widespread political loyalty. In this manner, a war which had commenced as a defensive struggle for national survival became a war of conquest and plunder.

In March 1796 Napoleon arrived in Nice to take command of the Army of Italy and embark on his long-planned invasion of the Italian peninsula. If the 35,000-strong army was short of both pay and equipment, it remained high in morale (**113**, Ch. 3). Its officers admired Napoleon's expertise and panache, as he quickly solved financial and supply problems by securing loans from Genoa. The Piedmontese were unenthusiastic allies of the Austrians, and French strategy was therefore to split the allies apart and knock the small Piedmontese army out of the war before attacking the more formidable Austrians (**69**, Ch. 4). Napoleon executed the strategy superbly. In April the Austrians were drawn forward into an exposed position to the south of their Piedmontese allies and then quickly pushed back to their base at Alessandria. As Berthier informed a friend in Paris, 'we do not march: we fly' (**86**, Ch. 5).

Before the end of the month Napoleon turned on the vastly outnumbered Piedmontese, defeating them at San Michele, Ceva and Mondovi before extracting from them the Treaty of Cherasco. This left him free to deal with the Austrians and move into Lombardy before attempting to thrust north through the Tyrol into Austrian territory. Such a strategy was very much Napoleon's personal one, for the Directory preferred to see the Army of Italy play second fiddle to Moreau's larger Army of the Rhine, which was to be awarded priority in a pincer movement against the Austrian Empire. In the eyes of the politicians in Paris, Italy was primarily a source of plunder, although it would also serve as a bargaining counter to be exchanged for territory in Germany in future peace negotiations with the Austrians. Napoleon had other ideas. The political significance of his Italian campaign lay in the fact that it was his policy that triumphed rather than that of his political masters; so much so that the relationship virtually became reversed.

By a brilliant flanking movement, Napoleon forced the Austrians to retreat in Lombardy. After battling across the bridge at Lodi, the French entered Milan on 14 May. This impressive series of victories, plus the loot and pillage which followed, further inflated the morale of the French troops and their willingness to fight and die for their gifted and dynamic young general. Such loyalty was reinforced by Napoleon's eagerness to plunder the riches of Italy and pay his men in silver rather than in depreciated paper currency. The waggon loads of loot despatched to France, together with the triumphant bulletins, increased his leverage with the regime in Paris, which now began to lose control over the young hero, especially when the political challenges from both the left and the right against the increasingly unpopular Directors rendered the government more than ever dependent upon its armies, in which Republican feeling was still strong, and upon spectacular military victories [**doc. 3**].

Realizing that it would prove impossible to force his way immediately into the Tyrol and Austria's under-belly until Moreau's Army of the Rhine moved east and deflected Habsburg forces from the Italian front, Napoleon marched south to occupy Bologna, Ferrara and Tuscany. With plundering French armies on their borders, the Papacy and the Kingdom of Naples hastened to sign alliances with their potential conqueror and pay substantial indemnities. At the end of May Napoleon turned northwards, towards the Austrian armies, aiming to capture the fortresses which guarded the Alpine passes and the route to Venetia and the Tyrol. The Austrians, having defeated the French armies on the Rhine and being unwilling to surrender their Italian territories without a fight, sent four armies down the passes in an attempt to dislodge the French and raise the siege of the fortress of Mantua. Napoleon defeated each army in turn: at Castiglione in August, Bassano in September, Arcola in November and Rivoli in January 1797 (**86**,

Chs 13–22). At these battles Napoleon displayed his skill in flexible manoeuvres and in moving troops rapidly; Augureau's division once covered seventy miles in two days. Early in February 1797 Mantua opened its gates to the French, who had become masters of Italy in less than a year.

Having grasped the importance of this series of dazzling victories achieved by the young Bonaparte and the threat which they posed to Habsburg power, the Directory now hastened to reinforce its Italian armies from the Army of the Rhine, as Napoleon moved up the passes towards Trieste (**100**, Ch. 13). By March the French had reached Klagenfurt, before pushing on to within sixty-two miles of Vienna. Here, with his soldiers exhausted, his lines of communication dangerously stretched, rumours of anti-French risings in Venetia, and still no offensive east of the Rhine by Moreau, Napoleon offered the Austrians preliminary peace terms at Leoben (**86**, Ch. 28). At the definitive Treaty of Campo Formio six months later, Austria ceded Belgium to France and recognized French rule over Bologna, Modena, Ferrara and the Romagna. The Venetian Republic was partitioned: the Ionian islands and part of Albania going to France, while the Austrians gained Istria and Dalmatia, as well as Venice itself. Napoleon therefore committed the Directory to territorial gains in Italy which marked a massive extension of the original Revolutionary war aims of achieving France's 'natural frontiers'.

Before the Treaty of Campo Formio, Napoleon had employed his considerable political and diplomatic skills to recast the structure of Italy. Austrian administration in Lombardy was dismantled. Modena, Ferrara, Reggio and Bologna were united in a 'Cispadane Republic' under French tutelage. Later in 1797 this was enlarged by the addition of Lombardy and some former Venetian territories and renamed the 'Cisalpine Republic'. This vassal state was given a system of government based on the French constitution of 1795, but members of both the executive directory and the two legislative councils were nominated by Napoleon himself, who attempted to steer a middle course between Italian democrats and conservative landowners. Such a policy led him, a former member of the Jacobin Club, to repress local Jacobin groups. Nevertheless, he was under no illusion about the nature of this *Realpolitik*, aware that his rule evoked little loyalty from the majority of 'liberated' Italians, who, given the chance, would be only too glad to see the back of pillaging French troops. Those who resisted the benefits of French liberty were summarily shot (**100**, Ch. 14).

In his reorganization of Italy, Napoleon virtually had a free hand, for by 1797 the Directory was in the throes of a major political crisis, the elections having returned a right-wing majority anxious for a royalist restoration. The prospect of a conservative regime in France encouraged the British to open peace negotiations. Both possibilities alarmed Napoleon, for a royalist restoration, no less than a general peace, would put paid to his burgeoning political ambitions. In September 1797 he therefore sent the Jacobin general Augureau to Paris to defend the three ex-Jacobin Directors, Barras, Reubell and La Revellière, from their right-wing colleagues and from royalist elements in the legislative councils. In the *coup d'état* of Fructidor, Augureau surrounded the Tuileries palace with soldiers, invaded the Councils, arrested the conservative Directors and invalidated the election of two hundred royalist deputies, before muzzling the opposition press. Hereforth the radical Republic survived as a mere rump, resting on the bayonets of its generals, while the politicians passed increasingly into the shadow of the awesome Bonaparte, whose victories not only sustained the regime at home, but also astonished and frightened Europe (**54**, Ch. 1). Napoleon had shrewdly employed his talent as a skilled publicist by sending his generals in relays to Paris during the Italian campaign to report his victories, not without some embellishment, and to lubricate the Paris press. In this manner the Italian campaign was transformed 'into a veritable Iliad' (**38**, Ch. 1). Napoleon himself returned to Paris like a conquering hero, handing over the Treaty of Campo Formio to the Directors in an elaborate public ceremony at the Luxembourg Palace. The *Institut de France*, Europe's leading scientific association, joined in the general hero-worship by admitting Napoleon to its mathematics section. Thus was born the Napoleonic legend [**doc. 4**].

After Campo Formio the name of Bonaparte had become as frightening to the Directors as it was to the Austrian generals, and they were quick to welcome Talleyrand's suggestion that an expedition to Egypt would deprive the young hero of a chance to meddle in political intrigues in Paris, with a powerful but idle army at his shoulder (**102**, Ch. 1). Napoleon himself was anxious to strike a blow against England and to fulfil one of his cherished dreams of oriental conquest, in which the acquisition of Egypt and a French empire in the east would mark the preliminary steps to ousting the British from India (**96**, Ch. 1). After inspecting the northern ports and naval dockyards, he became convinced that the French navy would be in no position to attempt a Channel crossing for some considerable time and that he would therefore stand a better chance of challenging British power by an expedition to the east.

In May 1798 a French armada of over 300 ships, carrying 35,000 soldiers and 150 scientific experts, sailed from Toulon and managed to avoid Nelson's fleet before capturing Malta. On 2 July Napoleon's 'Army of the Orient' disembarked at Aboukir Bay, bombarded Alexandria and marched across the desert to Cairo. Meanwhile Nelson reached the mouth of the Nile, caught the French ships at anchor and, displaying brilliant seamanship, blew them out of the water. This doomed the Egyptian expedition from the start, cutting it off from essential supplies and reinforcements. Nevertheless Napoleon pressed on, determined to exploit the tensions and divisions which existed in Egyptian society.

Nominally a province of the Ottoman Empire, Egypt had fallen under the feudal rule of the Mamelukes, who had originally been imported as slaves from the Caucasus, but now formed a military caste, much resented by the Egyptians. At the Battle of the Pyramids on 21 July, Napoleon crushed the Mameluke forces by employing defensive squares and deadly artillery fire (**67**, Pt iv). Proclamations were issued depicting the French as defenders of Islam and the Sultan, liberating Egypt from its enslavement to the Mameluke barbarians. Yet Napoleon had little success in persuading Muslim leaders to support the newly-installed French administration as an acceptable ally of Islam, rather than as the instrument of conquering infidels. The imposition of forced loans and heavy land taxes, as well as the ruthless crushing of all opposition, soon gave the lie to Napoleon's claims and provoked widespread revolts in Egypt, besides Turkey's declaration of war on France. The work of French scholars and scientists in founding libraries, laboratories and workshops, as well as making striking progress in tropical medicine, archaeology and Egyptology, failed to disguise the fact that the projected new colony rested on swords, muskets and cannon.

Although Napoleon's propaganda depicted the expedition as a dramatic and successful Oriental epic, with himself as the worthy successor to Alexander and Caesar, the Egyptian adventure soon turned sour. The British naval blockade made an imminent return to France impossible, so Napoleon decided to march into Syria in order to forestall a Turkish advance against Egypt. Syria soon proved a nightmare for Napoleon, who took a mere 15,000 men. His capture of Jaffa in March 1799 was sullied by his order to shoot

2,000 prisoners whom he could neither feed nor supervise. He then blundered by over-estimating the ease of capturing the fortress of Acre without heavy siege artillery. Acre was skilfully defended by Sir Sidney Smith's naval marine corps, and Napoleon, never at his best in siege warfare, was obliged to abandon his ill-planned assault and return to Cairo, after suffering losses of nearly fifty per cent [**doc. 7**].

After defeating a Turkish amphibious landing in Egypt, Napoleon resolved to desert his army and return to France. Newspapers, obligingly furnished by Sir Sidney Smith, informed him that Russia had declared war on France and invaded Italy, and that Jourdan had been defeated on the Rhine. On 24 August, therefore, Napoleon and a small entourage sailed for France. The army he had left under Kléber's command was eventually defeated in 1801 by Abercrombie's British force.

4 Brumaire

Napoleon landed at Saint Raphael in October 1799, acclaimed as the man who could save the Republic from its enemies at home and abroad. In his absence the war had been renewed, for Nelson's victory at the battle of the Nile had encouraged the formation of a Second Coalition of Turkey, Naples, Austria, Russia and England. Peasant risings forced the French to evacuate both Naples and Rome (**102**, Ch. 1). In April 1799 Suvorov's Austro-Russian army invaded Italy, occupied Milan and defeated Joubert at Novi. A Russian army advanced into Switzerland, while Archduke Charles smashed Jourdan's Army of the Danube at Stockach. In this perilous situation, the French were obliged to abandon Italy and prepare for a possible invasion of Provence. By the time Napoleon returned to France the military situation was improving, but the earlier reverses had damaged the already tattered reputation of the Directory and the political foundations of the Republic (**29**, Ch. 6). Many former supporters of the regime now began to argue for a stronger government in order to defeat the Coalition, eliminate the financial deficit and curb political extremism (**100**, Ch. 15).

The Constitution of 1795, designed to serve the interests of property owners who had done well out of the Revolution, had never operated satisfactorily and proved a source of constant conflict and instability (**103**). The strict separation of powers between the five executive Directors and the two legislative councils – the Council of the Ancients and the Council of Five Hundred – resulted in serious friction between the branches of government. Apart from this constitutional handicap, the Directory laboured under crippling financial burdens, exacerbated by economic stagnation, as it attempted to cope with a legacy of debt and inflation (**100**, Ch. 11). An increasing number of moderate deputies became pessimistic about the chances of the regime's survival, given the lack of any organized group which was firmly committed to republican principles and which possessed the energy and ability to prevent the growing desire for authoritarian rule (**104**, **101**, Ch. 6).

The exclusion of legally-elected deputies and government attempts to pack the councils with its own supporters created widespread apathy among the electorate. By 1799 there existed an influential group of veteran politicians alarmed by the election of a large number of Jacobins and willing to abandon parliamentary government in order to prevent the Republic drifting to the left.

It was against this background that Sieyès, a hero of the Revolution of 1789 who became a moderate Director in 1799, actively sought a revision of the constitution which would break the political deadlock by strengthening the executive at the expense of the legislature. Such revision, it was hoped, would prolong the dominance of the *notables* and neutralize future Jacobin threats (**54**, Ch. 2). Searching for a general who was willing to employ military force in order to push through the revision and act as a barrier against both royalism and Jacobinism, Sieyès solicited Moreau. Having met with a refusal, he turned to Napoleon, who not only possessed the prestige of being 'conqueror of Italy and Egypt', but whose brother Lucien was the newly-elected president of the Council of Five Hundred. During the ensuing complex manoeuvres, Napoleon displayed considerable political cunning, as he rejected overtures from Jacobin generals eager to make him military dictator of a left-wing regime. Neither had he any intention of being the mere catspaw of Sieyès. On the other hand, Napoleon needed the support of the politicians, for only the 'consent' of the Councils could throw a cloak of legality over a political *coup* and his bid for personal power (**doc. 5**). He therefore quickly seized the initiative from Sieyès, assumed control of the troops of the Paris garrison and the parliamentary Guard, and persuaded the Councils to move out to Saint Cloud, five miles from Paris, where they could be more easily intimidated.

Yet his plans nearly failed because of his ineffectiveness as a public speaker and his nervousness among hostile crowds. When he attempted, in a halting speech, to threaten the Council of the Ancients with military force, he was interrupted by cries of 'down with the dictator' and 'you are acting illegally' (**54**, Ch. 3). He fared even worse at the hands of the Council of Five Hundred, as angry Jacobin deputies rained blows on him and he had to be unceremoniously rescued by the Guard. Lucien saved the situation by alleging that an imminent 'Jacobin plot' existed and by persuading the Guard that an attempt had been made to assassinate his illustrious brother. The Guard, which harboured little respect for politicians, rushed into the chamber with fixed bayonets and put to flight most of the deputies (**38**, Ch. 1). A semblance of legality was preserved by inducing a docile rump of deputies to confirm a decision to set up a new executive government, consisting of three 'Consuls': Napoleon, Sieyès and Ducos. There was no further resistance, for the bourgeoisie had deserted the regime, while the common people of Paris saw no reason to rise in defence of a constitution which consistently excluded them from political power. The Paris Stock Exchange, on the other hand, welcomed the *coup* by a substantial increase in the value of government funds (**100**, Ch. 16).

During the following month, the new Constitution of the Year VIII of the Republic was carried through. It provided a much stronger executive than even the vacillating Sieyès had envisaged and failed to mention popular sovereignty. The three Consuls were to hold office for ten years and be re-eligible. Napoleon himself became First Consul, the two others possessing a merely consultative role. There was to be universal suffrage, unlike the constitutions of 1791 and 1795 in which the vote had been restricted by property qualifications (**54**, Ch. 3). But this was window-dressing, for the suffrage was so indirect and limited in its function as to be of little real consequence. In practice, only 6,000 men of substantial property were eligible for national office. A Senate of sixty men was nominated by the First Consul and then itself selected from the 6,000 *notables* a Tribunate of a hundred members who could discuss legislation but not vote on it, and a Legislature of 300 which could vote by secret ballot, but not discuss (**108**, Ch. 1). Legislation itself was to be proposed by the Council of State (*Conseil d'Etat*) of thirty to forty men, hand-picked by the First Consul who acted as its president and was empowered to nominate all major central and local government officials, including prefects of departments and mayors of communes.

The gestures to democracy and republican principles in the new Constitution were therefore largely meaningless, for power rested securely in the hands of Napoleon himself and flowed from the top downwards. He could appoint and dismiss ministers at will. The principle of the separation of powers was preserved, with ministers appointed from outside parliament and unable to participate in the proceedings of either the Tribunate or the Legislature. A plebiscite in February 1800, claiming that the new Constitution marked the fulfilment of revolutionary principles, resulted in three million votes in favour and only 1500 against. Until elections could be held and lists of notables drawn up, Napoleon simply nominated all officials, drawing on the advice of Talleyrand and Cambacérès in order to select either moderates, royalists willing to rally to the new regime, or penitent Jacobins. It was the fulfilment of Robespierre's prophecy that the Revolution would be concluded by a Messiah in army boots.

5 Marengo to Amiens

Although Napoleon attracted much public support in 1799 as 'a man of peace', what the articulate sections of the French public meant by peace was 'peace with honour', as exemplified by the Treaty of Campo Formio. In other words, France was willing to make peace, provided she was able to retain substantial foreign conquests, especially in Italy. This was very much Napoleon's own attitude, although his concept of peace was, if anything, rather more elastic. When Austria rejected Napoleon's propaganda-inspired offer to make peace on the basis of the Treaty of Campo Formio, Napoleon began to extort forced loans from Genoa, Switzerland, and Holland in order to finance the creation of a large reserve army at Dijon and Lyon, designed to reinforce either Moreau's Army of the Rhine or Masséna's depleted Army of Italy.

Napoleon's strategic plan was to take advantage of French possession of Switzerland by making it the central pivot of the whole war front. A spectacular victory would be achieved by ordering Moreau to attack on the Rhine, while 40,000 of the reserve army would advance audaciously over the still-frozen Alpine passes with the aid of pack mules and sledges to carry the guns, the barrels of which were to be hauled in hollowed-out tree trunks over the ice. This force was intended to take Mélas, the Austrian general who was besieging Masséna in Genoa, by surprise, as it suddenly appeared in his rear (**69**, Ch. 8).

Although there was some delay in shifting so many men, guns and supplies across the Alps in April and May 1800, and the toil over the Great Saint Bernard was perhaps not worth the effort involved, the strategy worked as intended. Other French armies poured over the Mount Cenis, Little Saint Bernard and Simplon passes. Not only did Moreau push back the Austrians in the north, leaving him free to reinforce the French armies in Italy across the Saint Gotthard pass, but Mélas was taken very much unaware when a large army appeared to the east of his own force (**53**, Ch. 1). Napoleon had already entered Milan, supplied his army from the fertile Lombard countryside as in 1796, and received reinforcements from the Army of the Rhine. After defeating an Austrian corps at Montebello, he advanced against the main Austrian forces near Alessandria.

At the battle of Marengo on 14 June 1800, Napoleon came within a hair's breadth of defeat. He made four major errors: only employing half his available forces in Italy; not moving against the enemy with his usual speed; sending three divisions away from the main army to carry out an encircling movement; and failing to undertake sufficiently thorough reconnaissance of the exact Austrian position and the state of the bridges in the area. The consequence was that the main Austrian army of 30,000 men and 92 guns suddenly appeared in the path of the French, having crossed bridges which Napoleon assumed to have been destroyed. Against this Austrian force, Napoleon could pit only 22,000 men and 15 guns, as he sent off frantic messages recalling the dispersed divisions. When Desaix reached the battlefield at three in the afternoon with one of these divisions, the main French army was already in confused retreat (**88**). A swift counter-offensive was mounted, in which Desaix advanced to his death at the head of his infantry, taking the now over-confident Austrians very much by surprise. Marmont procured eighteen guns to concentrate in an offensive battery, while Kellerman's charge with 400 heavy cavalry achieved the crucial breakthrough which led to a French victory and the loss by the Austrians of 3,000 men (**67**, Pt v).

Mélas consequently agreed to an armistice, whereby he was obliged to evacuate Lombardy and retreat to the fortress of Mantua. Desaix's appearance on the battlefield of Marengo had saved both the day and Napoleon's reputation. Napoleon's tactic of dispersing his forces and then quickly concentrating them near the enemy always carried a risk of the enemy attacking before the concentration was complete; this was a weakness his opponents were to exploit when they became familiar with his methods. Not surprisingly, the glowing bulletins issued in Paris failed to convey an accurate picture of what had happened at Marengo, which was depicted as a carefully planned and perfectly executed spectacular victory. It was at this time that the phrase 'to lie like a bulletin' became common among French cynics [**doc. 8**]. Nevertheless, Napoleon's defeat of the Austrians and his recapture of Lombardy enormously strengthened his position in France.

Austria, still linked with Britain by treaties and subsidies, and by no means subdued by defeat at Marengo, was slow to make peace. Indeed, further campaigns in Italy and on the Danube were necessary. It was Moreau's decisive victory over the Archduke Charles at Hohenlinden in Bavaria in December 1800, as well as pressure on Francis II by the Tsar of Russia, that eventually forced Austria to the conference table (**90**). By the Treaty of Lunéville in February 1801, France regained a somewhat expanded version of her acquisitions at Campo Formio, while Austria recognized French possession of Belgium and Luxembourg. The Treaty of Lunéville marked the end of the Second Coalition, as the Tsar exasperatedly withdrew his forces from western Europe (**89**).

Napoleon immediately embarked on a ploy to induce the Russians into an alliance against Britain, especially when the British capture of Malta in September 1800 offended Tsar Paul, who himself coveted the island, and caused him to revive the naval allliance of the Armed Neutrality of the North (Russia, Denmark, Sweden and Prussia) against Britain. This posed a threat to Britain's vital corn imports from the Baltic region (**92**). But Napoleon's hopes were dashed when Nelson destroyed the Danish fleet at Copenhagen in the spring of 1801 and the Tsar himself was assassinated. However, Pitt was willing to take up Napoleon's offer of peace negotiations and an exchange of prisoners. Britain was weary of constant warfare, as her economy began to feel the effects of the struggle, especially after deficient harvests and the collapse of textile markets, leading to outbreaks of popular disorder (**148**. Ch. 4). On the Continent there seemed little prospect of successful campaigns against the French, and when Addington succeeded Pitt as Prime Minister he continued the peace negotiations. On 1 October 1801 the preliminary Treaty of London was signed, on terms rather more favourable to France than Britain. These were only fully ratified in March 1802 at the Peace of Amiens, largely because Napoleon wished to delay as long as possible the French evacuation of Egypt, despite Menou's surrender to a British army in March 1801 (**29**, Ch. 7).

By the definitive Peace of Amiens, England was to return Egypt to Turkey, the Cape of Good Hope to Holland, and Malta to the Knights of St John; retaining only Trinidad and Ceylon from her colonial conquests. France pledged the evacuation of Naples and undertook to guarantee the independence of Portugal and the Ionian Isles. Each side, however, remained wary of the other. Napoleon had no intention of restraining his expansionist ambitions: England was still unwilling to accept French hegemony on the Continent (**54**, concl.) In France, the enormous prestige which Napoleon derived from the peace settlement gave him the opportunity to silence all opposition. He was now able to push through a plebiscite declaring him Consul for life, and to increase his power by the revision of the Constitution of 1799 and changes in the electoral system. No Bourbon monarch ever attained such absolute power.

How far the Consulate marked a sharp break with the Directory is a matter of some dispute. French Marxist historians like Georges Lefebvre and Albert Soboul saw the Revolution as coming to an end with the *coup d'état* of Brumaire in 1799, which extinguished parliamentary sovereignty and the genuine elective principle, making any kind of constitutional opposition extremely difficult. In theory the nation was still sovereign; in practice it was no longer consulted (**25**, Vol. i, Ch. 4). For those *notables* who valued their economic and social gains more than political participation, there was no major dislocation between the Directory and the Consulate. Napoleon retained most of the Directory's administrative machine and skilled bureaucrats (**105**). A good many of his most trusted officials had been members of the great Revolutionary assemblies, and now proved willing to continue and consolidate the economic and social modifications in French society which had begun so dramatically in 1789. But for those who saw the French Revolution as encapsulated in 'the sovereignty of the people' and the Declaration of the Rights of Man, the Revolution was clearly over.

Part Two: The Expansion of Empire

6 Consulate and Empire

Personality

When Napoleon became First Consul in 1799 he was thirty-one years of age and in his prime. A fascinating question is how much the vast expansion of French power in Europe between 1796 and 1812 was due to the extraordinary talents of Napoleon himself, and how much was owed to the Revolutionary society which supported him. Nowadays it is unfashionable to place much emphasis on the influence of individuals on the course of history. Yet it is difficult to accept the view that, if Napoleon had not appeared, then there would have been somebody very much like him to express the 'underlying forces' in society. His complex personality was unique, while his military genius has never been surpassed.

As well as being a professional soldier, Napoleon was a skilled politician and publicist, having served a rigorous apprenticeship in the intricacies of Corsican politics and the factional struggles of the French Revolution. At the same time he possessed serious scientific and literary interests, being capable of conversing with leading scientists and having once drafted a romantic, if rather turgid, novel (**38**, Ch. 3). The range of his reading, even when on campaign, remains impressive. His unrivalled command of detail and excellent memory enabled him to become a first-class administrator, while his renowned energy, powers of application and legendary capacity for work remained with him from his youth until something of a decline set in after 1808. Capable of working an eighteen-hour day and astonishing subordinates by the range of his knowledge, he drove perspiring secretaries to distraction. It has been estimated that, over the fifteen years of his reign, he dictated some 18,000 letters and orders: an average of fifteen per day (**4**, Ch. 11). He frequently dictated to six secretaries simultaneously on every conceivable topic, from grand strategy to the curriculum of girls' schools. His desire to govern France himself, even when out of the country (about a third of his reign), was sustained by his unusual reserves of nervous energy and his almost mystical belief in his 'destiny' as a latter-day Prometheus, greater than Hannibal, Caesar or Charlemagne (**25**,Vol i, Ch. 3), [**doc. 2**].

There was a price to pay, for his physique proved unable to cope with the excessive demands made upon it over the years. Contrary to myth, Napoleon needed six hours' sleep, and the enforced cat-napping and sleeplessness of continual military campaigns took their toll (**67**, Ch. 2). His tendency to live on his nerves and attempt to repress his powerful emotions beneath a veneer of cool resolve led to several nervous crises akin to epileptic fits. Spasms of rage or hysteria kept breaking through his pose of calm, icy efficiency. At such times he could thrash servants, or even military subordinates, with his riding crop. Yet he also displayed a teasing sense of humour, with ear-tweaking reserved for his special favour-ites (**30**, Ch. 6). The tensions and pressures of his amazing career led to premature ageing. By the time of the retreat from Moscow he was corpulent, lethargic and suffering from various ailments. Piles and bladder trouble affected his judgement at both Borodino and Waterloo. After 1812 he was less flexible and incisive, less able to distinguish between the possible and the impossible; more prone to negative fatalism and irrational obstinacy which made him, corrupted by power, a shadow of his former self.

His personality was always many-sided. Sometimes he appeared coldly efficient, as he referred to the need for rulers to instil fear into their subjects [**doc. 14**]. But he was equally capable of exuding charm and inspiring genuine affection and loyalty among those who came into close contact with him. He certainly attracted intense loyalty from his soldiers, as he played skilfully on their desire for comradeship, military glory and recognition of their bravery. He was assisted in this respect by his excellent memory for names and faces, and by his habit of riding among his troops, especially on the eve of battle. Even when fortune turned against him, he was able to maintain his hold over the *grognards* ('grumb-ling veterans'); there was less unrest among French soldiers in the *Grande Armée* during the retreat from Moscow than in Wellington's army in the Peninsula (**82**, Ch. 4).

One side of his nature was cruel and vindictive. Enemies were rarely forgiven and those who challenged him were often punished with all the zeal of a Corsican vendetta. Yet his loyalty to family and friends was equally a result of his Corsican upbringing. Those who had helped him in his youth were rewarded with jobs and emoluments when he achieved power. His childhood nurse was present at his coronation. It was his keen sense of clan and family that led him to place his brothers and sisters on European thrones, while misguided loyalty to old comrades led to his over-indulgence of disloyal subordinates like Bernadotte and Murat, whose military talents he over-estimated. The paradoxes in Napoleon's character can be multiplied. Despite the splendour of the Imperial court after 1804, he himself led a rather abstemious life in private, eating and dressing simply, in a style far removed from that of the Bourbon monarchs. Reality differed markedly from the romantic, super-human portraits of him by artists like David, Ingres and Gros (**219**). No true Frenchman ate such hurried meals or drank watered-down Chambertin.

Government

Napoleon created a vast European empire. He also fundamentally reformed the institutions of France. After Brumaire, his authoritarian personal rule enabled him to silence the warring factions and bring men together in his service who would otherwise have been bitter political enemies. He had a shrewd idea of what was necessary after a decade of revolution: 'My policy is to govern men as most of them wish to be governed. It is in this way, I believe, that popular sovereignty is acknowledged'. Although there was always some opposition to his rule, he was able to convert the majority of Frenchmen from being citizens to being subjects, and to impose on them a political, administrative and judicial system which reflected his own taste for efficiency and uniformity. What may appear to modern eyes as rigid and oppressive, seemed to many contemporaries to be 'rational' and 'modern' (**52**, intro.).

'*République française*' headed official documents until the creation of the Empire in 1804 and remained on coins until 1808; but the Consulate amounted to a monarchy in fact if not in name. After Brumaire, Napoleon was studiously ambiguous, saying at different times 'I am the Revolution' and 'The Revolution is terminated' (**38**, Ch. 1). In some ways Napoleon was obviously the heir of the French Revolution: in other respects he was more reminiscent of the enlightened despots. Nobody had profited more than himself from 'the career open to talents', a principle he firmly preserved. Given the basis of his support among the peasants and the bourgeois *notables* who had profited materially from the land sales of the Revolution, there were certain fundamental changes of the Revolutionary decade which Napoleon dared not tamper with. Among these were equality before the law, the destruction of feudalism, the land settlement, the erosion of the privileged position of the Catholic Church and the alienation of its economic assets (**54**, intro.). On the other hand, Napoleon was unwilling to permit the exercise of political rights, arguing that successive political crises after 1789 had been caused by unrestrained political disagreements. His own clear preference was for authoritarian rule, even if it meant the revival of some disconcerting features of the *ancien régime*.

Napoleon's claim to embody the general will in his own person directly contradicted the fundamental principle of the French Revolution: popular sovereignty modelled on Rousseau's social contract. Even the device of plebiscites – which in reality offered little genuine choice and were often manipulated – was abandoned after 1804 (**52**, Ch. 1). From 1799 itself, Napoleon resolved to confine the Tribunate and the Legislature purely to financial and administrative matters. When the Tribunate voiced criticism of the peace treaties and the Civil Code of law, it was heavily purged in 1802 and survived as little more than a rubber-stamp for Napoleon and his ministers until its abolition in 1807. The Legislature survived only by maintaining a low profile and criticizing Napoleon's policies cautiously and sparingly (**108**, Chs 2-9). The Senate also turned out to be a servile body, whose members were paid ministerial salaries of 25,000 francs and proved markedly reluctant to bite the hand that fed them.

Restriction of the scope of representative institutions was paralleled by an assault on individual liberties, especially the expression of political dissent in public assemblies or in the press. In Napoleon's eyes, the press ought to function merely as a dutiful agent of the government's information and propaganda machine. After 1800 the number of political journals was reduced from seventy-three to thirteen. Those which survived were effectively muzzled by being starved of information and forbidden to discuss controversial subjects. Many of the articles in *Le Moniteur*, the official government newspaper, were written by Napoleon himself [**doc. 10**]. In 1809 censors were established and appointed to each newspaper; as Napoleon wrote to Fouché: 'the newspapers are always ready to seize on anything that might undermine public tranquillity'. Draconian measures in 1810–11 limited the number of newspapers in Paris to four, with only one permitted for each provincial department. Additional controls were placed on printing, publishing and theatre productions. From July 1803, all books had to be submitted to government censors before publication; soon afterwards, the faculty of moral and political sciences at the *Institut de France* was closed down. In these circumstances it was difficult for educated public opinion to express its views on the regime and its policies, or for middle-class liberalism to develop (**109**).

The fact that the Consulate and Empire was manifestly a police state was nothing new. Arbitrary imprisonment and executions were frequent during the Terror and the Directory, let alone the *ancien régime*. By 1814 there were, in fact, only 2,500 people in gaol for political offences, since the Napoleonic regime was more sophisticated in its methods than its predecessors. The device of house arrest was widely employed by prefects to curtail the activities of groups of militant Jacobins and former Terrorists, or over-enthusiastic royalists (**52**, Ch 1). Thorough surveillance stifled a good deal of dissidence. In 1814 a police bureaucrat asked: 'Without the ministry of police how would one know the movement of society, its needs, its deviations, the state of opinion, the errors and the factions which agitate minds?' The Ministry of Police, founded in 1796 and headed by the wily Fouché from 1799 to 1810, controlled the four regional police divisions and was responsible for the secret police (*sûreté*), censorship, prison surveillance, food prices and the money market, although prefects and the mayors of large towns retained separate police powers under the Ministry of the Interior. Fouché sent Napoleon a daily digest of information drawn from his subordinates, as his Ministry monitored public opinion and nipped opposition in the bud by the use of spies, *agents provocateurs* and extra-legal powers [**docs 11, 12, 13**]. Food riots were much less frequent than under previous governments, partly because of firm repression, partly because of the requisitioning of grain from all over Europe to supply and pacify French cities (**122**, Pt ii).

Napoleon's was a new kind of personal rule, breaking with the traditions of both the *ancien régime* and the Revolution. Even Robespierre never possessed such a degree of personal authority. Divergent views were tolerated only in the Council of State, chaired by Napoleon himself. Ministers were permitted no collective responsibility nor autonomous decision-making (**113**). The same was largely true of the prefects in the provinces. As Dacrès, Minister of the Navy, once commented: 'We are all accustomed to being led step by step and we don't know how to initiate major policy' (**52**, Ch. 1). The centralized authoritarian system of government set up by Napoleon may be seen as the expression of his own personality and beliefs, as well as stemming from the need to restore stability to France after the political oscillations of the Directorial period.

Less immediately understandable is the transformation of the Consulate into the Empire in 1804 when, in the famous ceremony at Notre Dame, Napoleon took the crown from the hands of the astonished Pope and crowned himself and Josephine (**119**). His motives were a mixture of the personal and the political. Pressure from his squabbling relatives, especially his ambitious sisters, combined with his own keen sense of family loyalty and his desire to found a personal dynasty (**54**, concl.). The renewal of plots on his life also prompted him to establish an hereditary empire which would legitimize the *coup d'état* of five years previously and silence the group of political critics gathered around Sieyès, the Tribunate and the Paris *salon* of Madame de Staël. The Empire also marked a bid for respectability in the eyes of the European monarchs, though in the event they continued to regard him as a *parvenu*. George III was distinctly unimpressed when Napoleon took to addressing him as '*mon frère*'; the British government always coldly referred to the French Emperor as 'General Bonaparte'.

The creation of the Empire, and later of the imperial aristocracy, was also intended as another conciliatory gesture towards the royalists. The right represented more of a danger than the left, for the ranks of the Jacobins had been decimated by house arrest, police surveillance and the apathy of the common people. But the royalists had to be granted concessions, such as the abrogation of laws against the relatives of *émigrés*, the readmission to France of most of the leaders of the royalist opposition of 1797, the conclusion of a truce with the rebels in La Vendée and above all, concessions to the Church which culminated in the Concordat of 1801, designed in part to prise the Church away from the royalist cause.

The Concordat

The religious policy of the Revolution had turned out to be a conspicuous failure. Since the Civil Constitution of the Clergy in 1790 there had been considerable numbers of Frenchmen, and many more Frenchwomen, who had refused to accept that the ideals of 1789 provided a sufficient programme for the regeneration of sinful humanity, or that salvation by politics alone had much to commend it (**116**, Ch. 5). The schism in the French church after 1790 had led to civil war. Napoleon had been brought up a Catholic, but his education in the principles of the Enlightenment had robbed him of all genuine religious conviction [**doc. 9**]. For him, the

Catholic Church was a useful instrument of social control: instilling morality, preaching subservience to lawful authority, and confining women to home and family. He realized that the existence of an unreconciled 'refractory' non-juring church, with anti-clerical towns often locked in conflict with the rural faithful, stoked the ambitions of royalists and sustained popular counter-revolutionary movements in La Vendée and other strongly Catholic regions.

The Concordat was therefore planned as a dramatic gesture of reconciliation: an essential part of Napoleon's aim of unifying the country and bringing together former enemies under the firm hand of Napoleonic government. A *rapprochement* with the Church would provide his administration with yet another agency of social control. It would also keep La Vendée relatively calm, while increasing French influence in Catholic Italy, Belgium and the Netherlands. Pope Pius VII, more flexible than his predecessor, let it be known that he very much desired official recognition of the Catholic faith by the government of the most powerful Christian nation, as well as the repudiation of the 'constitutional' Church which had sworn loyalty to the French Revolution. The ground for the Concordat was carefully prepared. Napoleon prescribed mourning for the death of Pius VI in 1799 and arranged a *Te Deum* of thanksgiving in Milan Cathedral for victory at Marengo. Delicate negotiations with the Papacy led to final agreement in 1801 [**doc. 8**].

The Concordat, implemented in 1802 in France and Belgium (where it survives), signified a triumph for Napoleon, despite the opposition of his generals and most of the politicians. The Pope and the Church recognized the French Republic, thus breaking the alliance between the Papacy and the legitimate European monarchs, as well as dealing a crippling blow to the cause of the exiled royalists. The Pope accepted that the reunited Gallican Church would be obedient to the state, and that the new bishops would be nominated by the government, subject to Papal veto. Parish priests would be appointed by the bishops, rather than being elected. Both bishops and priests would draw state salaries, but there was no question of the state maintaining the number of clergy which had existed at the end of the *ancien régime*. Before 1789 there were 60,000 secular priests: in 1815 there were only 36,000 (**55**, Ch. 3). Religious orders were not generally readmitted to France, while new parishes could be formed only with government permission. Both church services and ecclesiastical processions were subject to restrictive police regulations. The official restoration of Sunday as the day of rest was offset in the eyes of the

Papacy by Napoleon's willingness to tolerate Protestant worship and refusal to persecute Jews. Catholicism was to be officially recognized as the religion of 'the majority of Frenchmen' – not of all Frenchmen.

On the surface, both parties to the Concordat received considerable benefits. The Catholic Church in France was formally unified and acknowledged the supremacy of the Papacy. The subordination of the lower clergy to the bishops seemed to augur well for an alliance between an authoritarian Church and an authoritarian state. In practice, the Concordat failed to operate as smoothly as anticipated. The full integration of 'refractory' and 'constitutional' priests took place only after many years of conflict between the rival groups [**doc. 11**]. As the Gallican Church began to recover its confidence, so it found its dependence on the state more irksome, for the degree of government control to which it was subject seemed to reduce it, in Dansette's phrase, 'to the humiliating status of a public servant' (**115**, Ch. 7). The Church's loyalty to the regime, though useful to Napoleon, was always less than absolute; most prelates would have preferred a Bourbon restoration (**29**, Ch. 10; **55**, Ch. 3).

Plots and prefects

One of Napoleon's reasons for negotiating the Concordat was to isolate royalism by dissociating it from official Catholicism (**52**, Pt i, Ch. 2). Although the government pardoned *émigrés* willing to swear loyalty to the regime, even returning confiscated estates that had not yet been sold, it had no compunction about using the stick rather than the carrot against royalists who were unwilling either to forget or forgive and who insisted on regarding the Emperor as a vulgar usurper. Vendéan leaders were executed, despite the truce. Cadoudal, the Chouan royalist who, sponsored by the British, became involved in a plot which included Generals Moreau and Pichegru, was executed along with eleven of his fellow conspirators. Mere suspicion of involvement on the part of the young Duc d'Enghien caused Napoleon to have him kidnapped from neutral Baden and shot by firing squad, without a scrap of solid evidence being found to implicate him. This act of judicial murder shocked Europe, although it prevented further plots against Napoleon's life and scotched rumours that he was planning a deal with the Bourbons. The minority of royalists who remained unreconciled became increasing isolated, as did the minority of Republicans who were unable to stomach the symbolic bees, flying eagles and other paraphernalia of the Imperial Court, and the attempts of official artists and propagandists to depict the Empire as a worthy successor to the great dynasties of history.

The group most loyal to the regime was the bourgeois property-owning classes (**143**). At the very beginning of the Consulate, Napoleon took steps to consolidate their support by decreeing that the interest on government stock be paid on time and in cash. The value of both the stock and Napoleon's reputation consequently rose in the eyes of the stockholders. In his negotiations with the Papacy, Napoleon made it clear that there could be no question of a restoration of church lands. What the propertied classes desired from the Consulate and Empire was stability and order at home and military victory abroad. Internal stability would safeguard their property against any threat from the left: victory abroad would prevent a successful counter-strike by the European monarchies which would involve the restoration of church and *émigré* property. Military victory and territorial expansion also provided lucrative opportunities for military contractors and suppliers, as well as an essential supplement to the domestic budget. Thus, despite the authoritarian nature of Napoleonic government, there were thousands of well-educated men, many of them former Republicans, or even Jacobins, willing to serve in the state bureaucracy and help to keep the country in the grip of its master. A considerable number of these willing participants had previously served in the administration of the Revolution, the Directory, and even the *ancien régime*.

The firm hand which Napoleon kept on the country was largely exercised through the prefects, themselves controlled by the powerful Ministries of the Interior and Police. These ministries were responsible for population policy, conscription, food supplies, commerce, poor relief, prisons, mines, public works, education and internal security. There were also ministries of Justice, Finance, Treasury, War, Navy, Colonies, Religion and Foreign Relations. Each was welded to the others in a centralized bureaucracy under the direction of the Council of State and of Cambacérès and Napoleon himself (**113**). The prefects, as the agents of the central government in the localities, formed the link between Paris and provincial administration. They executed the orders of the minis- tries and circulated government propaganda in the interests of Napoleon's version of the public good (**52**, Pt ii, Ch. 1). Prefects had to monitor public opinion, keep an eye on educated men who might develop dangerously independent views on government policy, supervise all clubs and associations and report suspicious activities. Prefects also had the task of implementing unpopular policies, such as installing new 'constitutional' *curés* after the Concordat – a procedure which often provoked riots – or assessing and administering unpopular taxes. Most important of all, they were responsible for the system of conscription at the local level and for checking desertion from the army [**doc. 28**]. If necessary, the central government could be called upon for assistance by semaphore telegraph, as when 4,000 soldiers were despatched from Paris in 1812 to quell major food riots in response to an alarmed appeal by the prefect of the Calvados department. A military tribunal sentenced eight rioters to death and seventeen to long terms of imprisonment (**122**, Pt ii).

The more positive side of the prefects' activities included compiling statistics for the ministries in Paris, supervising sub-prefects and magistrates, selecting local administrative personnel, presiding over local functions, taking steps to stimulate the regional economy and regulating food supplies, markets and prices. Most of the prefects were able administrators. Many of the later ones began their career as young *auditeurs*, who sat in on the meetings of the Council of State and were attached to the ministries as part of their training for the higher civil service. The creation of an administrative hierarchy, based on merit and open to the sons of the old nobility and the comfortably-off bourgeoisie, helped consolidate the regime and ensure the emergence of a loyal group from hitherto conflicting elites. The administrative system turned out to be Napoleon's most permanent legacy and survived in France until very recently.

The law

Equally firm control from the centre was exercised over the judiciary. Apart from justices of the peace, all magistrates were nominated for life, in contrast to the Revolutionary decade, when they were elected. Close supervision of the salaries and promotion prospects of judges helped to ensure their subservience to the government (**54**, Ch. 3). A repressive dimension was added to justice by the creation of 'magistrates for public security' and special tribunals for political offenders.

Since 1789 revolutionary governments had planned to codify and simplify the chaotic legal system of the *ancien régime*. In 1800, after firm pressure from the First Consul, the Council of State embarked on this herculean task, basing its approach on schemes drawn up earlier by Revolutionary and Directorial Commissions. In the Council's final draft, however, there was a marked reaction in favour of Roman law against the Enlightenment jurists of the Revolutionary period who had advocated, for example, equality between the sexes, civil marriage, inheritance by illegitimate children and equal division of property among heirs. Hence many features of the new Civil Code rejected the liberalism of the Revolution (**30**, Ch. 4).

Under the Code of 1804 the rights of individual property were confirmed, but the *ancien régime* despotic authority of the father over his wife and children was restored. A husband could have an adulterous wife or a rebellious child imprisoned. Illegitimate children were not awarded rights of inheritance. Although divorce was still permitted, it was made a difficult and very expensive process. Women were ascribed inferior status: 'a husband owes protection to his wife; a wife owes obedience to her husband'. A wife could be divorced for adultery, but she could divorce her husband on the same grounds only if he insisted on bringing his mistress into the household. This revival of the double standard marked a reaction against the liberalism of the Revolutionary decade, as well as an expression of Napoleon's own hostility to any kind of women's liberation and his belief that traditional family life strengthened social discipline and promoted public tranquillity (**54**, Ch. 3). Although the Code was the work of professional jurists, it was Napoleon himself who took the initiative in forcing it through, as he presided at thirty-six of the eighty-four sessions devoted to the subject by the Council of State. The authoritarianism of the Civil Code was mirrored in the subsequent legal codes. While equality before the law was more or less preserved, the Criminal Code and the Penal Code were rooted more in the *ancien régime* than in the Revolution. Perpetual hard labour and branding were restored; trial by jury was severely circumscribed; the *lettres de cachet*, which had facilitated arbitrary imprisonment before 1789 and outraged early Revolutionaries, were unashamedly revived in 1810. Special prisons for political offenders proliferated, especially with the spread of disillusion and disaffection after 1812.

Education

Napoleon was interested in schemes of educational reform, not only as a means of moulding minds and forming opinions, but also as a source of highly-trained civil servants (**54**, Ch. 3). However, his interest was largely confined to the education of the sons of the propertied classes. The common people, seen as needing no more than a simple 'moral education', were left with their traditional infant and primary schools, run by the Church, the municipalities and private individuals. No scheme of universal primary education was developed.

In practice, therefore, there were strict educational limits to 'the career open to talents'. Napoleon's government gave priority to providing a high-grade general secondary education, followed by professional instruction, for the sons of *notables* in the thirty-four *lycées* (highly selective and militarized boarding schools) established in 1802. The Imperial University was founded in 1806 as a kind of Ministry of Education, charged with the organization of public examinations, control of standards and curricula, the licensing of teachers, and the diffusion of a modern, scientific and practical culture among the sons of the élite (**55**, Ch. 3).

This system of state education enjoyed only limited success. The majority of bourgeois parents preferred to send their sons to private schools, usually those run by the Church, despite Napoleon's imposition of high taxes and irksome regulations on such establishments. The Imperial University functioned largely as a mere extension of the *lycées* (**134**). Advanced scientific education and research was conducted outside the University, in the *grandes écoles* founded during the Revolution. The most important of these was the *école polytechnique* (1794), whose intensive two-year course led to the specialized schools of mines, roads and bridges, or the artillery. Students then proceeded to high posts in the civil service or armed forces. In its early years, almost half the students were sons of peasants and artisans, supported by state scholarships. But in 1805 the Imperial government increased the fees and began the transformation of the *Polytechnique* from a major scientific university into a military school under the aegis of the Ministry of War, with the best pupils forced into military careers. Despite Napoleon's attempts to promote strictly utilitarian and vocational education, the scientific research which persisted at the *Collège de France* and the

Museum of Natural History enabled France to maintain her primacy in European science, while the arts continued to flourish in the private schools and colleges. (**52**, Pt ii, Ch. 2).

The Church

One reason why Napoleon's attempt to impose a uniform, state-controlled, quasi-military secondary education had only limited results was the resistance of the Church, which proved not quite so pliable an instrument for sustaining the regime as he had anticipated at the time of the Concordat. During the early years of the Empire, the Church was reasonably co-operative. The 'Imperial Catechism' of 1806 placed Napoleon on the right hand of the Deity, while the 'Feast of Saint Napoleon' officially replaced the traditional celebration of the Assumption of the Virgin. The bishops, once described by Napoleon as 'prefects in purple', obligingly prescribed a *Te Deum* for victory at Austerlitz in 1805, as well as helping to operate the system of conscription. The Bishop of Touraine urged conscripts 'to view their call-up as ordained by God'. Deserters and draft-dodgers were refused absolution.

Yet the Church was too powerful an institution for Napoleon to control at will. Part of the price which had to be paid for its role in maintaining tranquillity among the common people was its increasing influence in education, which eventually equalled that achieved under the *ancien régime*, The Church came to possess a virtual monopoly of private education; the teaching orders were revived; the *lycées* and the Imperial University were penetrated by tutors, inspectors and administrators in holy orders (**134**, Ch. 5). An Ultramontane spirit began to develop among the French clergy. Pius VII had accepted the Concordat only as second-best, and conflict between Pope and Emperor arose over the *Code Napoléon*, particularly its retention of divorce. It was exacerbated by the encroachment of French troops on Papal territory in Italy in 1805, leading to the occupation of Rome in 1808 and Napoleon's annexation of the Papal States. The rupture of relations came when the Pope excommunicated Napoleon and was promptly arrested and imprisoned by the outraged Emperor (**117**). Yet Napoleon always acknowledged the spiritual (as distinct from the temporal) primacy of the Papacy, and the quarrel does not appear to have cost him the loyalty of most French Catholics. Even the clergy only moved into opposition after 1812, when there seemed to be a real possibility of a Bourbon restoration.

Finance and economics

The new system of administration established under the Consulate enabled the government to tap the wealth of the country more effectively than during the *ancien régime* or the Revolution. The collection of taxes was made the responsibility of paid officials under the supervision of central Treasury officers and the prefects in the provinces. Firmer controls were placed over expenditure, leading to the balancing of the budget by 1802. A shift of emphasis from direct to indirect taxation was exemplified in the quadrupling of taxes on tobacco, alcohol and salt between 1806 and 1812, while the land tax remained no higher in 1813 than it had been on its introduction in 1791. Taxation policy was a further example of the regime distancing itself from the egalitarian principles of the Revolution in the interest of substantial property-owners. Industrial and commercial profits were taxed only lightly. Napoleon honoured the national debt inherited from the Directory and created new discount banks and a sinking fund to launch government stock and enable the state to pay its obligations to domestic creditors.

Until 1806 these financial measures and the confidence generated among the business and propertied classes enabled the state, assisted by financial regulation of the Bank of France, to keep the budget in balance and to finance its wars without the inflation of the currency which had crippled previous governments since 1789 (**52**, Pt ii, Ch. 3). The wars themselves brought substantial benefits. Plunder became a key aspect of government policy. It not only helped finance war and feed troops, but it also assisted the regime to become more firmly established and popular in France; booty from the war fronts stimulated French industry and agriculture and was important in keeping employment high and prices low. During the later years of the Empire, however, as the supply of loot began to dry up, military spending began to account for forty to sixty per cent of national expenditure. This had to be met by increases in taxation and customs revenue, which helped to deepen the financial crisis of 1810 (**146**). Even so, Napoleon's financial system remained much sounder than those of previous regimes.

Although substantial fortunes were made in the cotton industry, economic progress in general was unspectacular (**142**, Vol. i). While some historians detect a period of growth and expansion between 1800 and 1810, others, like Crouzet, argue that such 'growth' was merely a redressing of the economic decline of the

Revolutionary decade (**145**). There was certainly no far-reaching agrarian or industrial revolution. Compared with Britain, there was a significant lack of industrial and commercial innovation (**55**, Ch. 1). Agriculture remained traditional in its methods, expansion taking the form of an extension of the cultivated area rather than the introduction of new techniques. Prevailing high agricultural prices tended to support traditional methods of cultivation and husbandry, except in Alsace, Normandy and the Nord (**52**, Ch. 7; **38**, Pt iii, Ch. 3). The experience of the commercial sector was variable. Large-scale maritime commerce was largely destroyed by the British naval blockade so far as the Atlantic trade was concerned. Bordeaux, for example, which had suffered terribly during the Revolution, made something of a recovery under the Consulate, before being devastated again by blockade and the effects of the Continental System. Some parts of Aquitaine were effectively de-industrialized. The maritime economy of Nantes, based on the slave trade, was similarly ruined. Marseilles, on the other hand, was able to expand and draw on the Italian and eastern markets, while Strasbourg became a great merchanting centre, based on the German and Levant trade (**169**, Ch. 5).

There was more significant progress in the industrial sector, although it tended to be slow and patchy, especially when affected by the great European cyclical depression of 1810–12 (**38**, Pt iv, Ch. 6). While it is true that the French Empire at its peak provided a vast market for French products, domestic demand remained relatively inelastic. The slight rise in agrarian incomes tended to be offset by declining real wages in many industrial areas, as well as by the effect of higher indirect taxation. Moreover, the still primitive state of communications prevented the emergence of a truly national market and preserved a basically regionalized and fragmented economy. The most striking technical innovations took place in the cotton industry, with the spread of mechanized spinning and weaving in the Rouen, Lille and Mulhouse regions (**38**, Pt iii, Ch. 3). Developments in theoretical and applied science, especially in the application of sulphuric and hydrochloric acids, accelerated progress in the chemical industry; for example the creation of plant for the production of artificial soda in the Bouches-du-Rhône department (**52**, Ch. 7). By contrast, there was little technological innovation in the metal industries, where methods (including the use of charcoal in furnaces) remained traditional. But the demands of war obviously increased the scale of the iron and steel industries, leading to the establishment of new firms

in Languedoc and Marseilles, as well as in the Belgian departments. While the ministries and prefects did all they could to
promote economic development, many of the changes which took
place were merely extensions of trends which had appeared before
1800. A widespread industrial revolution and take-off into sustained growth, on the British model, had to wait until the reign of
Napoleon's nephew after 1851.

7   The Social Foundations of the Regime

Napoleon damped down political conflict and dissent not merely by repression, but by drawing into the service of the state men of talent from all factions and parties. State service provided channels of upward social mobility which were not entirely dependent on levels of wealth, though they were always linked with landed property at some stage. Bergeron's analysis of the 7,000 *notables* who formed the backbone of the regime reveals that a *notable* was generally a man of mature years, belonging to a professional group which conferred moral prestige, or possessing authority derived from office-holding or economic power from landed or commercial wealth (**141**). Napoleon used personal patronage to ensure loyal servants and to consolidate his rule, drawing many of his key personnel from the ranks of those who had served him in Italy or Egypt, including the scientists. He also promoted prefects who revealed high ability, as well as some *notables* and prelates more distinguished by their birth or wealth than their ability, but nevertheless useful as social cement.

The background of the prefects was diverse. Fifty per cent came from the pre-1789 nobility, the rest sharing a middle-class or military background. Some owed their appointment to the patronage of the Bonaparte or Beauharnais families or to the influence of their relatives. Most of them had been members of the Revolutionary assemblies, from all shades of the political spectrum, and possessed administrative experience at a high level. Napoleon's reintroduction of honours and decorations, abolished in 1789 as inegalitarian, was intended as a further means of binding men to his service and promoting loyalty to the regime. Swords of honour awarded to distinguished soldiers conferred double pay; sashes of honour were bestowed on loyal mayors. In 1802, on Napoleon's own initiative, the Legion of Honour was founded. The fact that only five per cent of the *légionnaires* were civilians reflected the growing ascendancy of military values (**38**, Pt iii, Ch. 4). After 1804, favoured members of the Senate were appointed to *sénatoreries* (national estates) and became super-prefects over a whole region,

40

with an urban seat, a residential palace and revenues of 25,000 francs a year.

The Imperial court and nobility were created between 1804 and 1808. Here again, the lion's share went to the military. Eighteen marshals of France were created in 1804 as 'Grand Officers of the Empire', receiving massive fiefs and revenues of between 500,000 and a million francs. Only four of them (Ney, Murat, Lefebvre and Augureau) were of lowly origin. Three had inherited or acquired nobility before 1789 (Davout, Berthier and Kellermann), while the others came from various sections of the bourgeoisie. After 1804 further feudal trappings were introduced, like the creation of fiefs in Italy after 1806 and in the Grand Duchy of Warsaw after 1807 for eminent *notables* (**52**, Pt iii, Ch. 2).

The re-establishment of a complete hierarchy of princes, dukes, counts, barons and knights emerged only after 1804. In order to become a prince or a duke an income of at least 200,000 francs and a record of outstanding service to the state was required. The first duke, for example, was Marshal Lefebvre, son of a police clerk and married to a former washerwoman, who became Duke of Danzig. Murat, son of a Gascon innkeeper, went one better and became King of Naples. Ministers, senators and archbishops could qualify to become counts; bishops and mayors were eligible for baronies. In all, about 3,600 people held titles of some sort between 1808 and 1814 (**162**, Pt iii, Ch. 1). However, the Imperial nobility was much smaller than that of the *ancien régime*, amounting to about fifteen per cent of the number of nobles in 1788. Entailed estates developed only slowly. Jean Tulard has demonstrated that the military accounted for seventy-nine per cent of the Napoleonic nobility, followed by higher state officials (twenty-two per cent). Men of bourgeois birth made up fifty-seven per cent, the old nobility twenty-three per cent and men of humble origins twenty per cent (**137**). In 1807 Napoleon told Cambacérès, himself created Duke of Parma, that the Imperial nobility was 'the only means of uprooting the traditional nobility'. It was also, of course, intended to impress foreign rulers.

Many people clearly did very well indeed out of the Napoleonic regime. As well as titles, the Emperor lavished gifts of land and money on 6,000 loyal supporters. His sister Pauline received 1,490,000 francs and the château of Neuilly; Marshal Berthier got almost as much money, married a Bavarian duchess and became Prince of Wagram. High posts in the civil service could be very well rewarded. In 1811 the income from all sources of the prefect of the Rhône department reached 63,000 francs (**52**, Pt iii, Ch. 2). Very few men could earn as much from industry or commerce. High state office invariably conferred more landed property; much valued at a time when commercial enterprise was relatively risky and unstable. The complex hierarchies of the Napoleonic civil service therefore offered lucrative opportunities to a middle class which was being progressively deprived of its revolutionary character.

While further research is needed on the common people of Napoleonic France, it appears likely that they benefited much less than those above them in the social scale. Upward mobility among agricultural labourers was very restricted, although a few managed to procure small-holdings in some regions of France. Rural artisans only began to join the ranks of the petty capitalists after the Restoration. Urban wage-earners seem to have earned more after 1800, largely because of acute labour shortages. But industrial discipline was savage; workers could be fined, placed under police supervision, or even imprisoned by their employers. The illegality of workers' combinations was reiterated in 1803. Successful strikes, like that of the stone-cutters employed on the Louvre in 1805, were very unusual. There was less unemployment among the labouring classes than under the *ancien régime*, but the improvement can easily be exaggerated unless the burdens of conscription and increased indirect taxation are taken into account (**55**, Ch. 3).

In a police state, with close surveillance and special tribunals for political dissidents, opposition was very difficult (**128**). It was made no easier by the apathy and powerlessness of the common people since the vicious repression of the *sans culotte* risings of 1795. At the same time, the bourgeoisie was politically emasculated, as the more able and educated became absorbed in the state bureaucracy. Yet support for the regime in the first plebiscite in 1800 was by no means as overwhelming as the government pretended. Nearly two million abstained, while the voting figures themselves were partially cooked by the Ministry of the Interior. Those who voted '*oui*' were probably more like half the official figure of three million.

Overt and organized opposition was much more hazardous and infrequent than voting with one's feet. At the centre, only a small group of Paris *Idéologues*, linked with a small opposition group in the Tribunate and with the independent journal *Décade philosophique*, was able to mount significant criticism of government policy (**127**). But this failed to persist, as opposition politicians were soon purged and confined to the enclosed and relatively harmless circles of the political *salons*. The bulk of the intellectual élite had been seduced by government patronage, while the *Idéologues* themselves lacked contacts with popular opinion, for by this time the common people had little regard for either intellectuals or politicians (**52**, Ch. 4). Organized opposition was otherwise restricted to plots and conspiracies, mainly by royalists who were able to rely upon a network of agents and contacts with foreign governments built up during constant counter-revolutionary activity since 1791 (**125**). Yet they never stood much chance against Fouché's Ministry of Police, with its swarms of spies and informers (**55**, Ch. 3). Opposition which centred on small underground groups, often composed of Italian immigrants, was of little more than nuisance value to the authorities.

The mass of the people never became involved either in organized political opposition or in genuine displays of enthusiasm. A regime which came to power in 1799 largely because it seemed to promise domestic tranquillity proved able to provide it only in urban areas, where an efficient apparatus of repression was combined with supplies of bread at controlled prices to local markets in times of general dearth [**doc. 6**]. But disorder in the countryside could never be repressed, especially during the economic slumps of 1805 and 1818–12, which led to vagabondage and brigandry on a massive scale, some organized bandit gangs being as large as a thousand men (**122**, Pt iii). Desertion from the army and resistance to conscription were the most characteristic forms of popular opposition to the regime. After Wagram in 1809 the wars began to lose their nationalistic appeal for many Frenchmen, as the armies became more cosmopolitan and pay fell into arrears. Draft-dodging had been widespread since the wars began in 1792, reaching a peak in 1799–1800 of thirty-seven per cent of men recruited from all parts of France. The national figure ran at twenty-seven per cent from 1801 and thirteen per cent for 1806–10, before soaring to a level in 1813 that represented a massive haemorrhage. The government's response alternated between the velvet glove and the mailed fist. There were five general amnesties between 1800 and 1810, for example. But more frequent use was made of the dreaded 'flying columns' to capture deserters, who then faced the firing-squad, or ten years in the hulks of Toulon or Antwerp. Accomplices were liable to heavy fines, five years' imprisonment, forced labour in irons, or drafting into barbarous disciplinary units at Walcheren or Belle Isle (**132**, **133**).

Although the propertied classes, including many of the old nobility as well as the bulk of the bourgeoisie, rallied to the Empire in order to secure social stability and resist the challenge from both the left and the right, the regime never in fact succeeded in attracting deep-rooted, unswerving loyalty, even from the *notables*. This was especially apparent after 1812, in a nation exhausted by continual warfare. Once Napoleon ceased to be victorious, the edifice began to crumble rapidly [**doc. 26**]. In 1814 the Napoleonic regime in France collapsed virtually overnight. The allied armies faced no major popular resistance movement when they marched over the French border. There was no Danton in Paris, as in 1792. Only the soldiers, especially the junior officers and members of élite corps like the Imperial Guard, remained loyal in 1814 and again in 1815. Marshals and generals were more concerned to preserve their estates and their fortunes. As Marshal Lefebvre commented in 1814: 'Did Napoleon believe that when we have titles, honours and lands, we would kill ourselves for his sake?' (**31**, Ch. 3).

8   The Humiliation of Austria and Prussia

The Peace of Amiens lasted only just over a year, never amounting to more than a temporary truce. During the peace, Napoleon maintained the exclusion of British goods from French and French-controlled territories, dashing the hopes of British merchants and manufacturers. Although French troops were withdrawn from Naples and the Papal States, Napoleon delayed the evacuation of Holland, annexed Piedmont and Elba, occupied Parma, forced Genoa and Tuscany to become vassal states and imposed a French alliance and French army on Switzerland. In response, the British refused to evacuate Malta at a time when the activities of French agents in the Middle East aroused suspicions that Napoleon intended a reconquest of Egypt. British support for royalist plots and the scurrilous attacks on Napoleon in the British press, much of it subsidized by the Government, also provoked the French. Britain was prepared to accept France's 'natural frontiers', provided that French expansion stopped at the Rhine, Alps and Pyrenees. But it was not in Napoleon's nature to accept limitations on French influence and territorial gains (**147**, Ch. 11) [**doc. 10**].

When hostilities were resumed in May 1803, Napoleon proceeded with his plan to invade England. Flotillas were assembled and deep harbours constructed at the Channel ports. Two thousand vessels of various kinds, including flat-bottomed barges, were intended to transport 100,000 men of the 'Army of England' (**149**, Ch. 4). But Napoleon soon discovered that only a small proportion of his armada could sail on any one tide, making it an easy target for the numerically superior British ships-of-the-line. An attempt was made to get round this problem by having Admiral Villeneuve sail to the West Indies and lure the British fleet across the Atlantic, before quickly doubling back and seizing control of the channel long enough to cover an invasion of England. The British Admiralty, however, guessed what was going on and retained a fleet in home waters which was eventually able to force Villeneuve's ships into Cadiz. Realizing that there was now no prospect of an immediate invasion, Napoleon ordered his troops, quickly renamed *La Grande Armée*, to strike camp on 24 August 1805 and march for the Danube.

Two months later Villeneuve, ordered to run the British blockade of Cadiz, had his Franco-Spanish fleet destroyed by Nelson and Collingwood off Cape Trafalgar. British superiority was partly a consequence of Nelson's genius and partly of the British navy's experience of constant naval combat since 1793. By contrast, the French navy lacked battle experience, having been thrown into confusion and neglect during the Revolution and then concentrating on blockade-running and the avoidance of offensive tactics. Between 1793 and 1814 the French had 377 ships-of-the-line captured or lost in action: the British only ten. After Trafalgar, British naval superiority was overwhelming.

While the French were being humbled at sea, they were triumphant again on land. Napoleon's march to the Danube in 1805 was provoked by the creation of a Third Coalition against him. The young Tsar Alexander was incensed by the French annexation of Hanover and Naples and the extension of French influence in Germany. He was also suspicious of Napoleon's designs on the Turkish Empire, where he harboured ambitions of his own. Austria, though plagued by economic problems, was outraged by Napoleon's establishment of the Kingdom of Italy in May, when he was enthroned in Milan with extravagant ceremony; the Iron Crown of Lombardy was traditionally viewed as the prerogative of the Holy Roman Emperors. Napoleon's annexation of Genoa, in flagrant violation of the terms of the Treaty of Lunéville, seemed further confirmation of his intention to deprive Austria of her foothold in Italy. Meanwhile the Tsar's growing hostility towards France led to the Anglo-Russian Convention of April 1805. When Austria adhered to it in August, the Third Coalition was in being, prompting Napoleon to march across the Rhine in an attempt to stifle the alliance at birth.

Assuming that Italy would be the chief theatre of war, the Austrians concentrated most of their army south of the Alps under Archduke Charles, sparing only 60,000 men under General Mack to await Russian reinforcements in southern Germany. But Napoleon's strategy was to relegate Italy to a sideshow, Masséna being ordered to pin down Austrian forces there in a mere holding operation. The Austrians played into Napoleon's hands by fatally underestimating the weight and speed of his advance into Germany; hence their failure to await substantial Russian reinforcements, which were following on behind Kutusov's advance force.

Napoleon's preliminary planning and staff work were meticulous: those of the Austrians confused and incompetent. The *Grande Armée*, advancing at 19 to 23 kilometres a day in seven separate, flexible army corps, each with a broad swathe of country to pillage, was the finest force Napoleon ever commanded. It contained a high proportion of hardened veteran regiments, as well as 286 field guns from French and Italian arsenals: a result of Marmont's efforts after 1800 to strengthen the artillery arm and place it at the hub of the battlefield. The size of the army, nearly three times that commanded by Napoleon in Italy in 1800, marked a significant escalation in the scale of warfare (**69**, Ch. 10).

At Ulm, on the Danube, the Austrian army expected Napoleon to advance from the Black Forest. Instead he wheeled round to the Austrian rear in a huge flanking movement, reinforced by Bernadotte's army from Hanover. Mack, finding himself suddenly surrounded, was obliged to capitulate on 20 October with 33,000 men. However, much to Napoleon's annoyance, the wily Kutusov and his Russo-Austrian force got away by a fighting retreat (**67**, Pt vii). Although Napoleon entered Vienna and was able to replenish his army from Austrian stores and arsenals, he was in an exposed position, with lines of communication stretching 1,450 kilometres from Paris. It was vital for him to persuade Prussia to continue the neutral stance she had adopted since 1795, as a Prussian assault on his flank would have been fatal. Fortunately for the French, King Frederick William resisted the increasing pressure from his bellicose Queen Louise and the vociferous war party in Berlin.

Despite Kutusov's advice that it would be better to wait until all available Austrian and Russian forces had combined together in overwhelming numbers before attacking the French, the Tsar and Francis II fell for Napoleon's ruse of a feigned retreat and moved forward against him. On 2 December 1805 Napoleon turned his army towards the Austro-Russian force at Austerlitz. Here he fought his greatest set-piece battle, with 73,000 men against an allied force of 87,000. His strategy of tempting the Austrians and Russians to stretch out their forces on a broad front, and then ordering Soult's corps to seize the Heights of Pratzen and cut the allied force into two, led to a dramatic victory, emphasized by the divided and confused enemy command. In this 'Battle of the Three Emperors', the Austrians and Russians lost 12,000 killed or wounded and 15,000 taken prisoner. French losses amounted to 8,000. The news of Austerlitz was received ecstatically in Paris and, like the news of Marengo in 1800, inflated Napoleon's popularity at home. Once more his bulletins were read out in village squares, by teachers in classrooms, and enacted on the stage (**31**), [**doc. 7**]. At the Treaty of Pressburg which followed the armistice, Austria was deprived of her remaining possessions in Italy and Germany, surrendering Venetia, Dalmatia, Istria, the Tyrol and Vorarlberg, while recognizing Bavaria, Württemberg and Baden as independent monarchies.

Although Prussia gained Hanover at the Treaty of Pressburg as a reward for her neutrality, Frederick William became alarmed in 1806 and found it more difficult to resist Queen Louise ('the only man in Prussia' according to Napoleon) and those in Berlin who demanded war with the French. Already he had been forced to surrender some territory and promise to exclude British goods from his kingdom. Napoleon's reorganization of much of central Germany into the Confederation of the Rhine also marked a challenge to Prussian power and influence. The Confederation arranged the various German states into large groupings of French client regimes, including the Grand Duchy of Berg, ruled by Marshal Murat, now married to Caroline Bonaparte. In return for the *Code Napoléon* and reformed administration on the French model, the Confederation was to supply Napoleon with 85,000 troops and substantial amounts of cash (**53**, Ch. 4).

It did not take long for French pillage and exactions to create an embryonic German nationalism, as well as irritating Prussia and provoking Austrian ambitions of revenge. Frederick William was not prepared to preserve Prussian neutrality at the cost of becoming a mere French vassal. What finally led Prussia to war were rumours that Napoleon was contemplating forcing her to hand back Hanover to England, as part of a peace package with the British. On 26 September 1806, Frederick William surrendered to the war party and sent Napoleon an ultimatum to evacuate his troops from all territories east of the Rhine. When the ultimatum was ignored, the Prussians, with their finances still in disarray and without waiting for the Russians to join them, embarked on a badly co-ordinated advance into Thuringia, designed to threaten Napoleon's force near Nuremberg and force them westwards.

In terms of numbers, the French and Prussian forces were equally matched, with about 130,000 men each. Otherwise they were grossly unequal. Only ill-informed German patriots believed that the Prussians had a good chance of victory. Their army, inactive since 1795, had become ossified, having failed to adopt the new developments in strategy and mobility which had made the

French armies so devastating. Prussian forces were still organized rigidly in unwieldy divisions, harshly disciplined, lacking initiative, attached to the old line-formation and restricted in their mobility by reliance on slow-moving and distant supply trains. Most of the general were aged veterans of Frederick the Great's campaigns: a gerontocracy wedded to the outmoded stately warfare of the pre-Revolutionary era. In advancing against Napoleon, rather than entrenching behind the Elbe to await Russian reinforcements, the Prussian army virtually committed suicide (**69**, Ch. 11).

Napoleon's strategy of a rapid advance on his enemy's rear, familiar by now to all armies but that of Prussia, threw Prussian plans into disarray (**55**, Ch. 2). His march from Bamberg to the north-east, threatening the Prussian lines of communication, caused the Prussians to retreat rapidly northwards to avoid encirclement. In southern Saxony they ran up against the French and gave battle. At Jena, Napoleon's army beat Hohenlohe's force, while nine miles to the north at Auerstädt, Davout routed the main Prussian army under Brunswick in an even more dramatic victory. Having lost 45,000 killed, wounded or taken prisoner, plus all their artillery, the Prussians were cut to pieces by Murat's merciless cavalry pursuit. As Chandler comments: 'seldom in history has an army been reduced to impotence more swiftly or decisively' (**67**, Ch. 43). As Napoleon entered Berlin to sleep in Frederick the Great's palace at Potsdam, Frederick William sought refuge with the Tsar at Königsberg (now Kaliningrad) 566 kilometres to the east. Victory over Prussia, soon occupied and partitioned by the French, marked a sudden and dramatic extension of Napoleon's empire, refuting those who had argued that he would be content to consolidate his gains in Italy and Germany.

9   Tilsit and the Continental System

Napoleon was unwilling to rest content with victory over Prussia. Although a peace treaty was drawn up, he refused to ratify it on the grounds that only a general peace settlement, including the return by Britain of captured French colonies, would satisfy him. Nor was Frederick William willing to make peace so long as there was a chance of Russia coming to his aid. The Fourth Coalition therefore remained in being. The French occupation of Prussia soon provoked Russian mobilization, which encouraged Napoleon to embark on a winter campaign in the bleak wastes of Poland in an attempt to bring the Tsar to heel. As well as raising troops from his German satellites, Napoleon persuaded 30,000 Poles to join him by hinting that, after liberating them from the Tsar, he might sponsor an independent Polish kingdom. Following an indecisive clash with Bennigsen's Russian forces at Pultusk, where both sides slithered ineffectively in the mud, Napoleon dispersed his army into the desolate Polish landscape to settle into winter quarters and await the spring. For the first time since 1796 he had failed to achieve his objectives in a single campaign.

The Russians, however, kept up the pressure by hit-and-run tactics and in February 1807 surprised the dispersed and outnumbered French forces by standing to fight in defence of Königsberg. At the battle of Eylau, fought in a snowstorm, neither side gained a clear victory. Napoleon failed to concentrate his army with sufficient speed, was guilty of slapdash reconnaissance and issued unclear orders to his subordinates. Although his 60,000 men managed to beat off 80,000 Russians and Prussians, they did so at a cost of 18,000 casualties and an inability to pursue the retreating enemy (**67**, Ch. 49). As usual, Napoleon's bulletins portrayed the battle as a famous victory, but Ney's comment was more apposite: 'What a massacre, and without result!' [**doc. 19**]. Suffering from nervous exhaustion, Napoleon consoled himself with seventeen-year-old Maria Walewska; but his army found no consolation in the fact that campaigning in eastern Europe in twenty-two degrees of frost was very different from fighting, pillaging and relaxing in the lush valleys of the Po and the Danube (**38**, Pt ii, Ch. 5).

Napoleon was now favoured, as so often, by disunity among his opponents. Not only did Austria fail to mobilize on his southern flank, but the Tsar and the King of Prussia quarrelled over strategy. Co-operation between Britain and Russia, poisoned by rivalries in the east Mediterranean, had become no more than lukewarm. Napoleon's position was also strengthened by levies of troops from the satellite states, which swelled the French army to 400,000, although only a thousand of the new soldiers were ready for front-line service. At the same time, the French supply problem, acute in such barren territory, was eased by the fall of Danzig (now Gdansk) and its valuable stocks of supplies.

In June 1807 Napoleon gained the decisive victory he sought over the Russians at Friedland (Pravdinsk), 43 kilometres south-east of Königsberg. Over 20,000 Russians were slaughtered or captured in a crushing defeat, which led to the capitulation of Königsberg the following day. The Tsar now sued for peace, secure in the knowledge that the French were not strong enough to march into Russia and impose vindictive terms (**69**, Ch. 12). Alexander and Napoleon met on 25 June on a pavilioned raft in the middle of the River Niemen. Impressed by the charm and flattery of the French Emperor, Alexander fell in with his plans to divide Europe into two great spheres of influence. The French were to retain their grip on western and central Europe, while Russian control was to be extended over Sweden, Finland and Turkey. The Tsar promised to apply pressure on England to make peace. In fact Prussia was the real victim at Tilsit. By the published treaty she lost her territories west of the Elbe and most of those in Poland, comprising a population of half a million. She was also to recognize the recipients of these territories: the satellite Kingdom of Westphalia and the newly-created Grand Duchy of Warsaw. The Prussians were to pay a large indemnity and restrict their army to 42,000 men. Russia lost only the Ionian Islands. In secret clauses, the Tsar promised war on England if she refused to make peace with France; while Denmark, Sweden and Portugal were to join Prussia in closing their ports to British goods (**186**).

Tilsit marked the zenith of Napoleon's career. On 27 July he returned to Paris after ten months in the field to a tumultuous hero's welcome of fêtes, parades and general adulation. Among his booty was the sword of Frederick the Great. The Napoleonic Empire now stretched from the Pyrenees to the Vistula: from the Baltic Sea to the Ionian Sea. Only Britain remained defiant, behind the wooden walls of her navy. Against this obdurate foe, Napoleon could employ only economic warfare, in what he characterized as a repetition of the struggle between Rome and Carthage [**doc. 10**]. The Continental System stemmed from two sources. It was partly an extension of French policy since the outbreak of war with England in 1793, when the Convention had decreed the exclusion of British goods from French markets. It was also a product of Napoleon's belief that Britain was on the verge of economic collapse [**doc. 20**]. In 1803 the Consular regime extended the exclusion of British goods to north-west European ports under French control. In November 1806 the Berlin Decrees declared Britain to be in a state of blockade, whereby all commerce with British ports was prohibited and all goods emanating from either British or British colonial ports were liable to seizure. When Napoleon gained control of the north German ports after Jena and secured the adhesion of Austria, Russia, Denmark, Sweden and Portugal to the Continental System after the Treaty of Tilsit, he was in a position to enforce the embargo on British goods more effectively (**25**, Vol. ii, Ch. 7). The consequent extra burden on the British economy would, he anticipated, lead to commercial surpluses and the draining away of bullion to pay for essential imports. This would cause economic collapse in Britain, followed by revolutionary upheaval (**169**, Ch. 1). These hopes were, in fact, based on a serious under-estimate of the resilience of both Britain's economy and her political system. While it is true, as Clive Emsley has recently demonstrated, that Britain's continued participation in the war 'put enormous strains on her government, her economy, her finances and her manpower', Britain's total exports held up between 1806 and 1814, while the threat of political revolution never materialized (**148**, intro.).

On the other hand, the Continental System caused great distress in Britain when it became fully operational. Unfortunately for Napoleon, the System could only be decisive in its impact if it were applied thoroughly over a long period. This proved impossible, for the effectiveness of economic warfare fluctuated according to French military fortunes. Whenever Napoleon's grip on the Continent was relaxed, European merchants rushed to counter the effects of French economic exploitation by importing large quantities of British goods. In the event, the Continental System could only be effectively applied between mid-1807 and mid-1808 and from mid 1810 to mid-1812. Otherwise it was seriously breached by the Peninsular War in 1808 and the renewed war between

France and Austria in 1809, before being dealt a mortal blow by the failure of the Russian campaign in 1812.

Before 1806 French measures against British trade enjoyed only limited success, as British and colonial goods entered Europe through Dutch and north German ports. Napoleon's troops marched into Poland in 1807 in Northampton boots and Yorkshire greatcoats (**67**, Ch. 44). But the effects of the Berlin Decrees were serious. Britain's immediate response was firstly to prohibit sea-borne trade between ports controlled by France and her allies; and secondly, by the Orders in Council of November 1807, to attempt to force all trade with France to pass through British harbours, thus preventing neutrals profiting at Britain's expense. Napoleon retaliated a month later with the Milan Decrees, whereby all neutral vessels calling at British ports, or submitting to British naval search, would be liable to capture and confiscation. These measures angered neutrals, especially the United States, already exasperated with the Royal Navy's practice of boarding American vessels and seizing British sailors who had joined American crews for higher wages. The Americans therefore issued an embargo on trade with both Britain and France, which had disastrous effects on British exports before it was lifted in 1809.

However, the situation improved for Britain when Napoleon's hold on northern Europe weakened as he campaigned against Austria. British goods immediately flooded into Europe. After Spain and Portugal were invaded by Napoleon, their South American colonies opened their markets to British goods. In an attempt to reduce the huge contraband trade via Gibraltar, Malta, Sweden and the Ionian Islands, Napoleon permitted limited imports of British goods under licence, in exchange for exports of French wines and silks. Victory at Wagram in 1809 made possible a reassertion of French control over European trade, with stiffer penalties for smugglers and more vigorous policing by detachments of the French army. The annexation of Holland, the Hanseatic towns and the Duchy of Oldenburg also facilitated the plugging of major holes in the system.

By 1810 the British economy was again in severe depression, followed by two years of commercial stagnation and social distress. But Napoleon's Continental System, though able to provoke severe dislocation, proved incapable of bringing Britain to her knees, given the limited period of full enforcement and the basic strength of the expanding British economy. Meanwhile economic warfare damaged the French economy as well as those of her enemies, especially when it resulted in a serious shortage of essential raw materials and a further reduction in the volume of French overseas trade. Even though the Continental System brought industrial and commercial prosperity to some regions, for example the Alsace and Belgian departments before 1810, it provoked considerable domestic resentment. Despite the fact that French finances remained strong, because of the more efficient system of taxation and the massive indemnities and confiscations Napoleon extorted from defeated powers and satellite regimes, French commercial and industrial interests remained dissatisfied. After the commercial and financial crisis of 1810–11 there was a marked decline in their enthusiasm for the regime, although the less impressive performance of the French armies no doubt played a significant part in their calculations (**169**, Chs 4–5).

The Continental System certainly caused serious discontent in the French Empire and can be linked with the growth of national resistance movements. It was designed not only as a weapon against England, but also as a means of ensuring French economic domination over the European Continent, especially in Germany. Before the 1806 Berlin Decree, France's economic primacy in Europe failed to match her military dominance. One aim of the Continental System was therefore to expand French industry and trade to the point where they would prove capable of filling the vacuum left by the expulsion of British commerce, by means of a rapid growth of French markets, stretching from Danzig to Bavonne, an area with a population of eighty millions. Yet the inherent weakness of the System was its one-sidedness, geared as it was to French interests and *la France avant tout* [**doc. 14**]. As Geoffrey Ellis writes: 'Just as Napoleon wanted political and military vassals rather than independent partners, so he wanted economic dependencies and tributaries, not competitive allies' (**169**, Ch. 3). Napoleonic Europe was not a free-trade area or common market, based on reciprocal favours and equal sacrifice to the common cause of defeating Britain; on the contrary, French industry and commerce were awarded special privileges and protection in a system of blatant economic exploitation [**doc. 18**].

The economic blockade disrupted the whole continental pattern of trade. Eastern Europe became choked with unsold cereals and timber; western Europe was deprived of sugar, coffee and raw cotton. Illicit British goods were publicly burned at Frankfurt at a time when French industry was unable to supply adequate substitutes. No European country possessed the administrative infrastructure to exercise thorough surveillance over the smuggling and blockade-running associated with the huge network of contraband traffic, which included France itself [**doc. 17**]. In August 1808 there were, for example, pitched battles between smugglers and customs officers in the department of the Doubs (**38**, Pt iv, Ch. 6). The growing nationalism which, especially after 1810, spread from the German and Italian intelligentsia to the mass of the people within the Empire, was partly a reaction to the burden of conscription and war taxation. But it was also sustained by the economic dislocation, unemployment, inflation and shortages which resulted from the imposition of the Continental System and the subordination of the economies of European countries to the needs of France. In the end, the Continental System was more trouble than it was worth, especially when Napoleon's desire to make it more watertight furnished him with one of the chief motives for his disastrous invasions of Spain in 1808 and Russia in 1812.

10 The Spanish Adventure

It was in 1807 that Napoleon set his sights on the Iberian Peninsula. Portugal was already a major nuisance to him, for the Portuguese government refused to subscribe to the Continental System, remaining loyal to the long-standing alliance with Britain and allowing the Royal Navy use of the Tagus and the ports. Napoleon accordingly prepared plans for an invasion force to advance through Spain into Portugal. Such plans also offered the opportunity for French interference in Spain, leading to its absorption into the French Empire.

Napoleon possessed only a superficial knowledge of the Iberian Peninsula. He never really grasped the problem of the sheer size of Spain (500,000 square kilometres), much of which was wild, empty and poor, and where living off the land was impossible. He wrongly assumed that both Spain and Portugal could be conquered and attached to his Continental System without much difficulty; and also erred in supposing that French ideas had general appeal in Spain. The urban middle-class *afrancesados* ('Frenchifiers'), who desired reform on the French model and despaired of achieving it under the decadent rule of Charles IV and Godoy, the Queen's favourite, were less numerous and influential than Napoleon imagined. The outbreak of the French Revolution had divided Spanish opinion and undermined the *illustrados*, a group of ministers and officials who had tried to modernize the monarchy and reinvigorate the state by loosening the immobility of Spanish society (**175**, Ch. 2). The Church and the majority of the propertied classes opposed revolutionary principles as atheistic and destructive of property rights (**179**). Under the pervasive influence of the priesthood, most of the population became strongly anti-French and hostile to those politicians in Madrid who embraced French ideas and schemes of reform (**176**, Ch. 2). During the decade prior to Napoleon's invasion, the conflict between traditionalists and modernizers, between 'Black' and 'Red' Spain, became more intense in a deeply-divided society whose crisis was aggravated by monks and friars crusading against French atheism and radicalism and by the ineffectual rule of the King and Godoy. Spain's weakness had already been revealed by her disastrous war against France between 1793 and 1795, which obliged her to seek peace and a French alliance, and which led to the British navy severing her from her colonial empire.

During the summer of 1807 Napoleon persuaded Godoy to co-operate in a scheme to partition Portugal, to provide soldiers and supplies and to permit French occupation of key Spanish fortresses. In November, Junot's army of 25,000 advanced through Spain towards Lisbon, but was prevented by popular revolts from fully occupying Portugal. In Spain, the doddering Charles IV was faced by a plot to have him deposed which had the support of his son Ferdinand and a network of French agents. Posing as a mediator between father and son, Napoleon summoned the Spanish royal family to Bayonne, forced Charles to abdicate and the strongly anti-French Ferdinand to renounce the succession. Joseph Bonaparte was proclaimed King of Spain, as a French army under the flamboyant Murat was sent to occupy Madrid and impose French rule (**161**, Ch. 7).

Such high-handedness revealed a serious misunderstanding of the attitudes of the Spanish people. Although many of the 'enlightened' intelligentsia welcomed French occupation, the majority of the population remained loyal to Ferdinand and transferred its hostility from Godoy to the French and to those sections of Spanish society which collaborated with the invaders. On 2 May 1808 the *pueblo*, the common people of Madrid, rose in revolt against Murat's savage Mameluke cavalry, killing 150 before being crushed. A series of mass executions followed. These events, unforgettably commemorated in 1814 by Goya in his two great paintings of 'The Days of May', provoked a massive wave of popular resistance across the whole country. The deep fissures in Spanish society meant that 'the war of liberation' was at the same time a civil war between pro- and anti-French groups, between liberal Spain and reactionary Spain, and even, in some places, between rich and poor.

The French now found themselves among a permanently hostile population, as Spain split into its component parts, each headed by a *junta* (resistance committee) of local clergy and notables. Mayors of villages organized ceremonious declarations of war on the French, in the name of King Ferdinand. Napoleon was forced to despatch 'flying columns' from his army of 120,000 in an attempt to pacify the country and damp down resistance. At Baylen on 19

July a French division of 9,000 raw recruits was encircled and massively outnumbered by 30,000 Spanish troops raised by the Seville *junta*, plus 10,000 irregular partisans, and forced to surrender. News of this first defeat of a French army in the field created a sensation in Europe and caused Joseph to withdraw all French armies north of the Ebro. Realizing that he now had a major war on his hands, Napoleon arranged a meeting with the Tsar at Erfurt and extracted a vague promise that Alexander would try to restrain Austria during France's embarrassment south of the Pyrenees. Napoleon himself then set off for Spain with 100,000 veterans from the *Grande Armée* in central Europe.

Faced by an invasion on this scale, the Spanish central *junta* in Cadiz appealed to Britain for aid and Sir Arthur Wellesley (later Duke of Wellington) duly disembarked in Portugal with a small army of 14,000 and defeated Junot's force at Vimiero in August 1808, although the French were allowed by the Convention of Cintra to evacuate Portugal. Soon afterwards Wellington was replaced by Sir John Moore, whose British army of 28,000 did its best to co-operate with the regular Spanish troops and the various irregular bands. Napoleon, with nearly 200,000 men massed on the Ebro, now deployed them in flanking assaults on the two main Spanish armies, intended as a preliminary to the recapture of Madrid. This strategy was foiled by Moore, who marched his army to the north and boldly attacked French lines of communication, drawing numerically superior French forces to the west and providing the hard-pressed Spanish armies with a breathing space, before embarking on a fighting retreat to Corunna (**180**, Ch. 2). Napoleon, realizing that Moore could not be prevented from escaping, and worried about Austrian mobilization on the Danube, left Spain early in January 1809, leaving Soult and Ney to pursue Moore. At the battle of Corunna on 11 January, the British lost 6,000 men, including Moore himself, but fought the French to a standstill before being evacuated by the British navy (**67**, Ch. 60). Moore had saved southern Spain and Portugal from immediate occupation and had ruined Napoleon's programme for the speedy subjugation of the Peninsula (**182**).

What Napoleon termed 'the Spanish ulcer' persisted to 1814 and engaged 250,000 French troops by the time he invaded Russia in 1812. Joseph Bonaparte was never more than the nominal ruler of a people in constant turmoil and revolt. Once Wellesley had returned to Spain, the French were unable to dislodge his army, always less than 30,000 strong, from its foothold in Portugal, sheltered by mountain ranges and fortified lines and well supplied by the British navy (**181**). While the French could easily handle the badly co-ordinated Spanish regular armies, irregular bands made it impossible for French forces to combine in sufficient numbers to oust Wellesley. Throughout Spain the French were plagued by *guerrillas* ('little wars'), a name soon applied to the bands of men who, having suffered disaster in open warfare, learned to operate by stealth, descending suddenly on enemy detachments and harassing lines of communication and supply, before melting away to the hills and the forests under cover of darkness. Although the guerrillas wasted some energy in squabbling with each other, they formed a crucial part of the national rising against the French invaders, in defence of the Church, the old order and the Bourbon monarchy. The French consequently became bogged down in a vastly enlarged version of La Vendée, whose horrific atrocities were starkly depicted in Goya's searing etchings of 'The Disasters of War'. Captured French soldiers were stoned to death, blinded with pikes, or left castrated and bleeding. The methods of the French were hardly more civilized.

Both Spanish regular warfare and guerrilla activity provided essential support for Wellesley, since they diverted substantial numbers of French soldiers. The French also suffered from divided command, since Joseph was not given overall control of French forces before 1812 and Napoleon's marshals tended to remain jealous of each other and unwilling to co-operate (**161**, Ch. 7). French armies in Spain became increasingly unenthusiastic about a war which seemed to lack purpose or to provide the opportunity to make tangible gains [**doc. 22**]. After his victory at Wagram in June 1809, Napoleon sent Masséna and 130,000 men to Spain in a bid to end the war. But Wellesley was able to move from behind his lines of Torres Vedras and repulse Masséna's army on the ridge at Busaco, where French losses of 25,000 revealed the superiority of the British lines of trained and disciplined riflemen over the massed French columns (**69**, Ch. 15). There followed a prolonged struggle for the fortresses controlling the Spanish-Portuguese border. Only in 1812 were the British able to capture Ciudad Rodrigo and Badajoz, before luring Marmont to defeat at Salamanca and entering Madrid in August. After briefly retreating in the face of superior forces, Wellesley was able to mount a decisive advance in 1813. His crucial victory at Vitoria forced the hapless Joseph, who lacked any talent for military strategy, to flee his ill-gotten kingdom, leaving Soult to deploy weakened armies in a doomed defensive campaign. Wellesley then pushed across the Pyrenees to Bordeaux, finally defeating the French at Toulouse in 1814 (**180**, Chs 4–6).

There is no doubt that the French invasion of Spain was a catastrophic error on the part of Napoleon. It proved a constant drain on manpower and resources and helped to encourage resistance to French rule in central and eastern Europe, besides blunting French morale and eroding the prestige of France's armies. The effort needed to hold back Wellesley in the Peninsula played an important part in crippling Napoleon's defensive campaigns in Germany and France in 1813 and 1814. The Spanish war cost Napoleon 300,000 casualties and untold quantities of gold and war materials. Arguably, the French could have won in Spain if Napoleon had been willing to assume permanent command there, which would have meant restraining his ambitions elsewhere in Europe. In the event, the Spanish war was never popular in France and became a factor in the alienation of the propertied middle classes from Napoleon and his regime [**doc. 12**]. As Talleyrand remarked to Alexander I at Erfurt: 'The Rhine, the Alps, the Pyrenees are the conquests of France; the rest is the conquest of the Emperor, not supported by France' (**38**, Pt iv).

11 Wagram and the Austrian Marriage

After her defeat at Austerlitz in 1805, Austria suffered much the same feeling of humiliation as Prussia after Jena in the following year. Napoleon's domination of Italy and Germany threatened the great-power status of the Habsburg Empire. The first step was to reform the army. Archduke Charles increased its front-line strength to 350,000, copied the French system of independent army corps, and created regiments of mobile skirmishers and sharp-shooters. Mobility was assisted by the adoption of a French-style supply system. Resistance to Napoleon's forces in Spain encouraged the Austrians to test whether he was capable of fighting a war on two fronts (**156**). Battle plans were drawn up in 1808 and news of them soon came to Napoleon's ears (**155**, Ch. 4). He decided to mobilize immediately, for Austria must not be allowed to move into southern Germany and northern Italy without opposition.

The French Emperor was now faced by a problem of manpower which was to plague him until 1815. In order to build up his forces to 300,000 in central Europe, he had to withdraw the Imperial Guard from Spain, consequently weakening the French effort there. As well as levying 100,000 men from the vassal states, he also called up over 110,000 French conscripts from the class of 1810. These measures reflected a major factor in the eventual downfall of the Empire: the declining quality of the troops under Napoleon's command, as the proportion of hardened native French veterans to raw recruits and non-French contingents began to decline. The *Grande Armée* in Germany in 1809 lacked the quality of that of 1805, much of it being little more than an untrained militia. In these circumstances the Austrians stood a good chance of beating Napoleon if they moved quickly enough. But although the Emperor Francis II decided on war in February 1809, he took military action only in April, when Archduke Charles's army of 200,000 moved from Bohemia into Bavaria without a declaration of war. The Austrian plan was to destroy the French forces in the Ulm-Augsburg region before the French cavalry had assembled and the Imperial Guard arrived from Spain. Another Austrian army under the Archduke John was to hold Italy. This strategy came near to succeeding, for Napoleon lingered in Paris, leaving command in Bavaria to Berthier, who, though a fine staff organizer, possessed no talent as a field commander. It was only when Napoleon himself arrived that the *Grande Armée* was able to gain the upper hand in a series of clashes in Bavaria, inflicting heavy losses on the Austrians without being able to destroy them or prevent their orderly retreat (**69**, Ch. 14). Napoleon was obliged to give chase and seek an overwhelming victory before the Prussians were tempted to come in against him.

On 12 May the French bombarded Vienna and then entered the Austrian capital as the Habsburg armies rallied north of the Danube. Napoleon, pushed into moving quickly before the Archduke John arrived from Italy with the other main Austrian army, now came to grief. Attempting to create a bridgehead across the Danube at the villages of Aspern and Essling, he seriously underestimated Austrian strength and found himself facing 115,000 men with only 82,000 of his own. The Austrians, by attacking first, took Napoleon unawares and pushed the French into a bottleneck, forcing them to retreat to the island of Lobau. Both sides lost 20,000 killed or wounded – a casualty rate as high as the worst battles of the First World War (**67**, Ch. 64). Although Napoleon did his best to disguise the fact that the battle of Aspern-Essling had been a clear defeat, news of the Austrian triumph sped round Europe, assisted by energetic Habsburg propaganda. But Napoleon had the acumen to settle down to six weeks' careful preparation and to await the arrival of substantial reinforcements before a second confrontation. Meanwhile the Austrians hoped for a general German rising against the hated French, and for Prussian mobilization. The Prussians, however, realizing that Napoleon was still full of fight, remained neutral while they awaited the outcome of a second French offensive, concentrating in the meantime on remodelling their army and administrative system.

By 5 July Napoleon was ready for battle. Archduke Charles took up a defensive position, with an over-extended front, based on the village of Wagram. There followed a savage two-day battle, very much a gigantic clash of artillery, before Napoleon finally gained victory by breaking through the Austrian centre. Although the Austrians were defeated, Wagram was not to be compared with Austerlitz or Jena. While the Austrians lost 40,000 men, the French in their turn suffered casualties amounting to 30,000 and the Archduke Charles was able to withdraw intact a force of 80,000 and demand an armistice. The Peace of Schönbrunn in October 1809 cost Austria three-and-a-half million subjects. Salzburg went to Bavaria, the Illyrian provinces to France, and parts of Galicia to Russia and the Grand Duchy of Warsaw. Austria also had to pay a large indemnity, restrict her army to 150,000 men and impose the Continental System throughout Habsburg territory. Yet there were encouraging signs for Napoleon's enemies. Austria had fought surprisingly well in 1809, proving able to match the hitherto unsurpassed French artillery. Some of the raw recruits in the French ranks had panicked and fled at Wagram, while Napoleon seemed less infallible after his setback at Aspern-Essling. There were indications that he could no longer maintain the intense pace he had imposed on himself in previous campaigns and that he was tending to overestimate his own skills and belittle those of his opponents. Moreover, it was widely remarked that he had been forced to station troops in Germany and the Tyrol to suppress local risings, which underlined the fact that the continued existence of the French empire depended on a succession of decisive military victories.

On the surface, Napoleon appeared triumphant again. Metternich, who replaced Stadion as Chancellor, calculated that a French alliance would best secure Austria's short-term interests (**249**, Ch. 2). Hence his moves to procure a dynastic marriage. Motivated by his desire for a legitimate son and heir, and shaken by a plot to replace him in which Talleyrand, Fouché and Murat had been involved, Napoleon had for some time been contemplating a divorce from Josephine. She had failed to bear him a child and was now in her forties. The birth of a son to Maria Walewska in 1807 convinced him that he was capable of fathering an heir. To make his able step-son Eugène his official heir would cause trouble, there being little love lost between the Bonaparte and the Beauharnais families. Nevertheless, Napoleon did not find divorce easy, for he remained fond of Josephine, despite the fact that she had been unfaithful to him soon after their marriage. Attempts to secure a match with one of the Tsar's sisters had come to nothing and, after much lengthy negotiation between Napoleon and Metternich, a marriage was arranged between the French Emperor and Marie-Louise, the rather empty-headed daughter of Francis II. Napoleon thereupon divorced Josephine, with the approval of the Archbishop of Paris if not the Pope, in December 1809. The chances of an heir seemed promising, for Marie-Louise's mother had had thirteen children, her grandmother seventeen and her great-grandmother twenty-six. The marriage between the French Emperor and the eighteen-year old Archduchess took place in April 1810, and was followed nearly a year later by the birth of a son, the King of Rome. Frenchmen must have been disconcerted to see the 'heir of the Revolution' married to a niece of Marie Antoinette. Certainly many staunch Republicans found the marriage repugnant [**doc. 21**].

Part Three: Decline and Fall

12 The Napoleonic Empire

By 1810 the French Empire in Europe stretched from the Tagus to the Niemen, from the Baltic to the Adriatic. Only Portugal, the Kingdoms of Sicily and Sardinia, Montenegro and the Ottoman and Russian Empires remained outside Napoleon's system of dependent or allied states. Russia was technically an ally after Tilsit, but was moving out of the French orbit as early as the Congress of Erfurt in 1808 (**227**, Ch. 2). Much of Europe was ruled directly from Paris: the Illyrian provinces and the Ionian islands, the duchies of Parma and Piacenza (annexed to France in 1806), Tuscany (1808), the Papal States (1809) and Holland (1810). There were also the dependent satellite kingdoms: Holland, ruled by Louis Bonaparte unitl 1810; Italy, under Eugène Beauharnais as Napoleon's viceroy; Naples, ruled by Joseph Bonaparte until 1808 and then by Marshal Murat, Napoleon's brother-in-law, as 'King Joachim'; and Westphalia, ruled by Jérôme Bonaparte. Spain, with Joseph on the throne from 1808, was never brought under French control and therefore hardly ranked as a satellite. Another exception was the Grand Duchy of Warsaw, officially governed by the King of Saxony, but regarded by Napoleon as a mere bargaining counter in diplomacy and as a military base. Other client states included Switzerland and the sixteen German principalities grouped in the Confederation of the Rhine. Denmark, Prussia and Austria had all been forced to ally with France.

The satellite kingdoms were primarily intended to provide Napoleon with troops, supplies and, above all, money. They were also intended to play their part in the enforcement of the Continental System [**doc. 14**]. At the same time, however, they were agents of political and social revolution, challenging the old regimes by fostering French principles of careers open to talent, the suppression of feudalism and local privileges, the abolition of serfdom, and the introduction of the *Code Napoléon* with its standardization of law, open courts and trial by jury. Professional administrations on the French model were also introduced in the satellite kingdoms, while the guild system and internal customs barriers were disman-

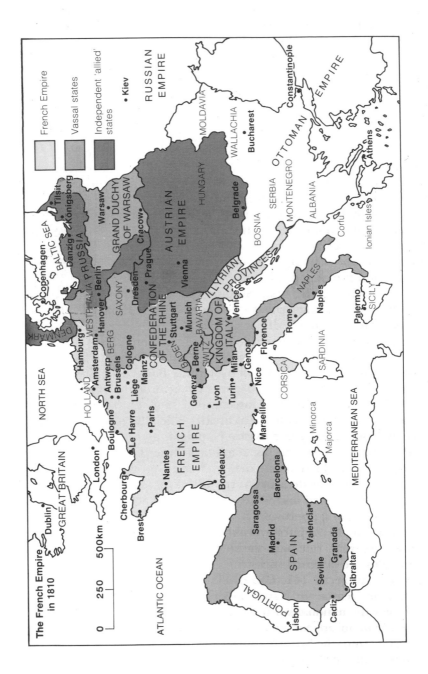

The French Empire in 1810

tled. Constitutions were granted which allowed a degree of participation in legislation and decision-making by a mixture of the old nobility and the new professional élites [**doc. 15**].

It seems doubtful whether Napoleon had a definite master plan for the development of Europe, but there are signs that by 1810 he was moving in the direction of a centralized empire, governed directly from Paris (**161**, Ch. 2). The early republics, which soon proved too independent for his taste, had been suppressed. The Ligurian Republic (Genoa) was annexed to France; the Italian and Batavian (Dutch) republics became kingdoms in 1805 and 1806. New monarchies were established in Naples, Westphalia and Spain. One reason for Napoleon's tightening of central control over the satellite kingdoms was because the members of his family whom he placed on thrones turned out to be less submissive than he expected, being averse to subordinating the resources of their territories, as well as their own popularity, to the interests of France and the exigencies of the Continental System. Only Eugène was completely loyal, besides being the most able and efficient of the clan. At the other extreme, Louis Bonaparte became strongly attached to his Dutch subjects, refusing either to introduce conscription or to impose more than a very mild form of the Continental blockade. Hence Napoleon's slow strangulation of Holland in 1810 and the forced abdication of Louis.

In Naples, the hot-headed and emotional Murat, manipulated by his ambitious and cunning wife, Caroline Bonaparte, ignored many of his brother-in-law's orders and promoted Neapolitan nationalism for his own dynastic purposes. Jérôme Bonaparte, able and courageous behind his facade of 'playboy king', provided Napoleon with the requisite cash and troops, but refused to enforce the Continental System in Westphalia with the thoroughness the Emperor demanded and was too respected by his subjects to meet with Napoleon's approval. It appears that, but for the Russian campaign in 1812, Jérôme would have gone the way of Louis. In Spain, Joseph's rule was thoroughly inept, and despite his high principles he aroused neither affection nor respect among his Spanish 'subjects' (**41**, Ch. 4).

Another reason for Napoleon's increasing control over the satellites was the national spirit which emerged in Italy and Westphalia and began to appear in Holland and Naples. This was certainly not something he wished to encourage, given his conception of a cosmopolitan empire based on ambitious middle-class groups anxious to sweep away the old regimes by embracing the Napoleonic version of the principles of 1789. That such groups might come to regard cosmopolitanism as a mere cloak for French national interests, and instead develop firm nationalist aspirations of their own, was something Napoleon hardly bargained for. A further factor in Napoleon's calculations was the Austrian marriage of 1810 and the birth of the King of Rome, which made him less reliant on his siblings. His son would, as his title implied, become the heir of a new, integrated Roman Empire. This helps to explain the acceleration of moves to annex more of Europe as mere departments of France, or as military governorships under Napoleon's direct control: the annexation of Holland and Hanover, the strengthening of the French garrison in Naples and the subversion of Murat's authority, the removal of nearly three-quarters of Spain from the hands of Joseph into those of military satraps. No doubt this process would have gone further but for the defeat in Russia and the consequent erosion of the military power which bound the Napoleonic empire together.

Although allied states like Prussia, Austria and the principalities of the Confederation of the Rhine hastened to introduce reforms on the French model, not least in their armies, it was in the satellite kingdoms that the most determined efforts were made to establish French patterns of government and administration. Eugène in Italy had the most successful record (**44**). Italians spent longer under French rule than other nationalities and perhaps felt a closer affinity with the Bonaparte family, which was Italian in origin. Only the Kingdom of Italy was able to maintain a balanced budget, under the essentially authoritarian rule of Eugène, despite the existence of a constitution. The Council of State was composed of Eugène's nominees, while the parliament was little more than a talking shop for men of property. Economic prosperity resulted from Italy's becoming a major centre for the lucrative trade between France and the Levant and for thriving contraband traffic. The balanced budget was a consequence of this economic prosperity and of rigorous tax collection. Feudal dues were abolished, the *Code Napoléon* was introduced, and the influence of the Church curtailed (**164, 165**). Eugène's government also reformed primary and secondary education and provided state subsidies for the universities and the arts. The army was expanded and remodelled, playing an important part in the Austrian campaign of 1809 and the Russian campaign of 1812, as well as being embroiled in Spain (**161**, Ch. 2).

The Kingdom of Naples was much less successful [**doc. 14**]. The gross inefficiency of its Bourbon rulers had left a permanent legacy. Corruption and passive resistance nullified the new central administration's efforts to collect taxes and stimulate industry and commerce. Little could be done about the vast gulf between rich and poor, or about the power of the Church in a country where ten per cent of the male population was in holy orders. The *Code Napoléon* could not be introduced in the face of overwhelming local resistance, while the army remained little more than a militia, dependent on foreign mercenaries. Murat, with his glamorous uniforms, gaudy ceremonies and colourful court was more to Neapolitan taste than the relatively dull Joseph, whom he succeeded as king in 1808 (**167**). But he was hardly more successful, for he was unable to operate the constitution bequeathed him by his predecessor, or to impose the Continental System in its full rigour. Murat's increasingly questionable loyalty to his Emperor led him to encourage Neapolitan nationalism, though to little effect, as rising taxation and heavier conscription after 1810 bred popular resistance, which culminated in guerrilla outbreaks in regions like Calabria (**161**, Ch. 4).

The Kingdom of Holland was a source of constant exasperation for Napoleon. The affable and generous Louis Bonaparte was anxious to serve the interests of his Dutch subjects so far as he was able. The Constitution of 1806 granted genuine political participation and permitted semi-autonomous provincial administration (**166**, Chs 1–3). In spite of Napoleon's entreaties, 'King Lodewijk' steadfastly refused to impose conscription, relying instead on Hessian mercenaries. By 1810 the Dutch army was only 31,000 strong and unable to forestall a British landing at Walcheren in 1809 without the assistance of 30,000 troops rushed from France. Even the mild version of the Continental System introduced by Louis proved devastating for a country which lived almost entirely by trade. Only illicit commerce and condoned violations preserved the economy from utter collapse. In 1810 Napoleon put strong pressure on Louis to adopt ruthless policies in order to clear the budget deficit and procure the cash and troops he constantly demanded from the satellite and vassal states [**doc. 16**]. Louis resisted the pressure, but he was eventually forced to abdicate and surrender his kingdom to direct French rule (**161**, Ch. 5).

Westphalia was very different from Holland. Stretching across northern Germany from the Weser to the Elbe, it was formed from territory seized from those German states which opposed the French in 1806–7. Napoleon intended it to be the anchor state of the Confederation of the Rhine and something of a showpiece, with its liberal, progressive constitutional monarchy and its reputation for industrial enterprise and fine soldiers. The Constitution of 1807 was carefully prescribed by the Emperor [**doc. 15**]. In return for providing an army of 25,000 men and bearing the costs of 18,500 French troops garrisoned on her territory, Westphalia was to enjoy religious toleration, equality before the law and the abolition of feudal rights. King Jérôme was to be advised by a Council of State and a parliament, though he possessed the sole right of proposing legislation and appointing officials. Despite his habit of by-passing parliament in order to meet the Emperor's demands for money and troops, and of using his large network of police and spies to stifle opposition, Jérôme became respected as a capable monarch (**43**). The *Code Napoléon* was a success and the judiciary and the courts were both reformed (**55**, Ch. 2). The Westphalian army drew upon an impressive military tradition, Hessian soldiers being renowned throughout Europe. The 25,000 troops raised by 1809 were of fine quality, for Jérôme introduced French strategy, weaponry and drill, besides opening up the officer corps to talent. The Westphalians were to distinguish themselves in the Peninsula and in the Russian campaign. By 1813, however, the Kingdom was exhausted and nearly bankrupt as a consequence of a soaring national debt and the stagnation of industry and commerce in a society geared almost totally to war (**161**, Ch. 6).

When Napoleon breezily informed his elder brother Joseph that 'in Germany, Italy and Spain, people long for equality and liberalism', he must have had his tongue in his cheek so far as Spain was concerned. In the eyes of the majority of Spaniards, as well as of Napoleon himself, Joseph's essential benevolence was viewed as weakness. His timidity in the face of Spanish armies and bands of guerrillas and his desire for easy popularity earned him the respect of neither the Spanish people nor French military commanders like Lefebvre, Jourdan, Marmont and Soult, who regarded him as a bumbling amateur. Programmes of economic, legal and administrative reform were consistently obstructed by 'Black Spain' at the local level. Spain was therefore a satellite kingdom in little more than name. The enormous costs involved in the attempt to subdue the Iberian Peninsula far outweighed the contributions of the other satellite states. It is hardly an exaggeration to conclude that Spain bled the Empire white (**161**, Ch. 7).

The French model of government and administration which Napoleon sought to develop throughout the Empire was very much that followed by all advanced 'modernizing' societies during the nineteenth century, with its principles of centralization, abolition of privileged groups, uniform codes of law and the extension of the power of the state over the lives and resources of citizens. Such a model appealed to the enlightened, upwardly-mobile middle classes, as well as to the military. It had, however, relatively little appeal for the common people, either urban or rural, of the Napoleonic Empire. They resented the increased taxation, the 'blood tax' of conscription and, above all, the creation of efficient police forces. The achievements of the satellite rulers in conferring civil and legal equality and embarking on programmes of economic development were counter-balanced by the subject populations' lack of choice in the matter. Enlightened reform was so much less attractive when it came from the barrels of French guns.

In the final analysis, Bonapartist rule was designed primarily to serve the interests of France and rested on force and military success. There was no way that European peoples would have accepted French hegemony of their own free will. The French presence was genuinely supported only by small minorities, like the *afrancesados* in Spain. Once Napoleon had been beaten in Russia, then French rule was rapidly shuffled off. Many of the middle classes, especially in Germany, embraced nationalism as a means of seeing the back of the French. Yet the peasants who composed the bulk of the armies which finally brought down the Napoleonic Empire fought not so much from nationalist feelings as from traditional loyalty to the Church and to the dukes and princes of the *ancien régime*, loyalties which Napoleonic government never succeeded in eroding. For most of the population of Europe, the 'war of liberation' from 1813 was a crusade of traditional conservatism against those who tried to impose reform on large numbers of people who had no wish for it, especially when it came in French garb.

On the other hand, the significance of burgeoning nationalism in Europe after 1808 should not be discounted, for it became widespread among intellectuals and the educated middle classes, especially in Germany (**193, 194**). Here the chief stimulus was the shock of Prussia's defeats at Jena and Auerstädt. As Meinecke wrote in 1905: 'A new sense of freedom and energy was spreading through society at the very time that the state had lost its independence' (**196**, Ch. 6). A deep sense of shame and bruised pride was instrumental in shifting the basis of the German Enlightenment from cosmopolitanism and rationalism to a more romantic and nationalist *Weltanschauung*. Cosmopolitanism had been so much more appealing when the French armies were at a safe distance. Thinkers like Schlegel, Fichte and Herder now began to emphasize the superiority of the German cultural tradition, based on the powerful concept of the *Volk*. This Romantic tradition, seen as owing more to emotion and religion than to reason and the principles of 1789, was cultivated as an essential source of resistance to French cultural domination and was to act as a vital stimulus to German national consciousness.

Prussian reformers after Jena were much more interested in resisting French armies than French culture, but were quick to harness the groundswell of German nationalist feeling exemplified in such patriotic writings as Fichte's *Addresses To The German Nation* [**doc.·27**]. Politicians and generals like Stein, Scharnhorst and Gneisenau were eager to launch English and French-style reform programmes, in order to end the ossification of Prussian society in the hands of the old aristocratic caste, which had proved fatal in 1806, and thereby revive Prussian military power and self-respect (**71**, Ch. 5). A series of reforms in Prussia, including the emancipation of the serfs, municipal self-government and restructuring of the fiscal system, helped to strengthen the Prussian state, as did steps towards economic liberalism. Within two years of Jena, the social and economic basis of Prussia was in the process of transformation, enabling her to resume her character as 'a compulsively regulated machine for producing revenue and soldiers' (**72**, Ch. 11).

The reorganization of government undertaken by Stein's reforming ministry after 1807 included a unified War Office and a Military Reform Committee, which aimed at the creation of a new national army based on patriotism and honour rather than the slavish obedience of the old Prussian automata. Citizen soldiers were to be recruited to supplement hardened regulars. Incompetent officers were dismissed. So were many aged commanders; in 1806, for example, the Prussian army had contained four active generals over eighty years of age and eighteen over seventy years. The military academies were also restructured. Young officers were selected by aptitude and merit from the sons of commoners as well as nobles. Such reforms were underpinned by an educational programme which provided more schools offering a modern practical curriculum. Draconian military discipline was relaxed, if only because it had led to massive desertions. As in Westphalia, French military tactics of mobility, flexibility and independent army corps were adopted to replace the cumbersome structure and rigid line-formation of the army of Frederick the Great. Exemptions from conscription were limited and the system placed on a fairer basis [**doc. 23**].

Until 1813 the size of the Prussian army was restricted to the 42,000 men stipulated by Napoleon after Jena and only cautiously circumvented by the government in Berlin. The new *Landwehr* (provincial militia), Prussia's answer to French mass conscription, was only fully mobilized and blended with the regular army, now increased to 65,000 men, during the winter of 1812–13. But the *Landwehr* could be rapidly expanded to provide 120,000 reserve troops, themselves augmented by the *Landsturm* (Home Guard). When Napoleon returned from Russia in 1812, there was a powerful Prussian mass army awaiting him west of the Niemen (**201**, Chs 4–5).

13 Russia 1812

The alliance between Napoleon and the Tsar, formed at Tilsit in 1807, was always brittle (**189**). Both rulers possessed distinct and antagonistic ambitions; each saw himself as the greatest man on earth, under the protection of a special 'destiny'. The alliance could have been truly cemented only if Napoleon had been willing to support the Tsar's designs on Constantinople; but the French Emperor, with Mediterranean ambitions of his own, was unwilling to pay such a price. There were other sources of friction between the two rulers. Napoleon's alliance with Austria and marriage to Marie-Louise offended the Tsar; so did France's retention of Prussian fortresses on the Oder, allegedly to cover Austria's northern flank, but also posing a threat to Russian territory. When Napoleon annexed the north German coast in 1810 in order to make the Continental System more effective, he also seized the Duchy of Oldenburg, in defiance of the Tilsit agreements, at a time when the Duchy was linked to Russia by the marriage of the Tsar's sister to the Crown Duke. Alexander was also worried by the enlargement of the Grand Duchy of Warsaw under the terms of the Peace of Schönbrunn between France and Austria. This seemed to revive the possibility of an independent kingdom of Poland, when Russia would come under pressure to restore the Polish territory she had acquired in the partitions of 1793 and 1795 (**186**).

However, the major bone of contention between Napoleon and Alexander was the Continental System. For Napoleon, it was not only a means of economic warfare against his most dogged enemy, the British, but also a demonstration to the courts of Europe of his personal ascendancy. In Russia, the imposition of the Continental System after Tilsit created commercial havoc, as capital drained abroad to pay for imports which could no longer be covered by Russian exports. As trade slumped, so did the exchange rate, followed by the rapid depreciation of the paper currency. In December 1810 the Tsar began admitting neutral ships to Russian ports and levying duties on French products, thus opening up one of the most massive breaches in the Continental blockade. Both

74

British and Prussian agents urged the Tsar to defy Napoleon, while the Russian nobility was becoming strongly nationalist, particularly when Speranski, the Tsar's chief minister, commenced a programme of unpopular administrative and tax reforms on the French model.

Infuriated by Alexander's casting aside of the Continental System, Napoleon in 1811 began diplomatic moves to isolate Russia. Although he gained support from Prussia and Austria, he received none from Sweden and Turkey. The French had invaded Swedish Pomerania when Prince Bernadotte, Napoleon's former marshal, refused to exclude all British colonial goods. The upshot was that Sweden sought an alliance with Russia, finalized in April 1812. In May the Turks signed the Treaty of Bucharest with the Tsar, freeing the South Russian Army to take up defensive positions on the western frontier. Nor was Napoleon able to rid himself of the Spanish ulcer, for Britain rejected the peace overtures of 1812, when the French offered to quit Spain if the British would acknowledge Joseph as king and withdraw Wellesley's forces. Nevertheless, Napoleon was determined to teach the Tsar a lesson which would demonstrate to both Britain and Europe the uselessness of defying French imperial power.

Yet from the very beginning the attack on Russia was a gamble, with the odds against the *Grande Armée*. It was simply too big. An army of that size could not be properly fed and equipped in the pre-railway age, nor could such a lumbering monster be deployed according to the mobile, flexible tactics of French Revolutionary warfare (**71**, Ch. 5). Napoleon gambled that the Russians would mount a large-scale frontal attack not too far inside their borders. When they failed to do so, they virtually sealed the fate of the *Grande Armée*.

During late 1811 and early 1812 Napoleon built up the *Grande Armée* in Germany to a total of about 600,000 men, as troops were summoned from all quarters of the Empire [**doc. 24**]. Not only did such a cosmopolitan horde present serious problems of language and discipline, but the reliability of a considerable proportion of it was also doubtful. Moreover, Napoleon's inordinate demands for military supplies from the allied and vassal states were never fully complied with; from the very first there was a crucial shortage of medical and other supplies. At Smolensk, the wounded had to be bandaged with straw, plus paper from the local archives (**191**, Ch. 5). In a summer of virulent epidemic strains, 60,000 men were on the sick list before the campaign actually opened.

Early in June 1812, Napoleon joined the advanced forces of the *Grande Armée* at Königsberg after attending a fortnight of parades, processions and celebrations in Dresden, designed to silence sceptics and overawe the crowned heads of Europe (**188**, Ch. 3). His strategy was to lure the Russian armies towards him, before splitting them apart and defeating them in turn. He calculated that it would require a mere nine weeks before he was in a position to dictate a Carthaginian peace to the Tsar. Facing Napoleon across the Niemen was Barclay de Tolly's First Army of 125,000 on the Russian right, and Prince Bagration's Second Army of 47,000 on the left flank, south of Vilna. The Tsar's unwillingness to appoint a supreme commander resulted in a good deal of friction between the Russian generals.

The French armies crossed the Niemen into Russia on 23 June. But Barclay avoided a pitched battle by retreating quickly to the east of Vilna, while Bagration managed to slip away from Jérôme's army in the south. It was not long before the route into Russia became a *via dolorosa*. The progress of the *Grande Armée* was painfully slow on poor or non-existent roads, while lines of stragglers stretched far back in the rear. Hundreds of horses died from the effects of eating unripe corn; one officer counted the carcasses of 1,240 along the 80 kilometre route from Kovno to Vilna. The commissariat broke down within a few days of crossing the Niemen, and by the time the front-line troops reached Vilna the baggage trains were far to the rear. Insects, diarrhoea and hunger laid men low. Although Napoleon realized that it would be very difficult for such enormous forces to live off the land, they were soon obliged to do so. Nor were supplies forthcoming in Vilna where the Lithuanians turned against the French as a result of looting and Napoleon's refusal to announce a restoration of the Kingdom of Poland (**184**, Ch. 2).

Barclay abandoned plans to make an early stand against the French, preferring to wait until Bagration's army was able to join him. Davout prevented the junction taking place at Vitebsk and the two Russian commanders were only able to unite their forces at Smolensk, a mere 450 kilometres west of Moscow. This marked a success for the French, in that the Russians finally combined forces much further east than they had intended. On the other hand, the Russians had been careful not to provide the French Emperor with the early set-piece battle he so desperately needed. In Moscow Alexander proclaimed a 'national war of resistance in defence of

Mother Russia', to continue so long as the *Grande Armée* remained on Russian soil (**187**, Ch. 9). By the time that Napoleon's forces reached Vitebsk, they were so strung out along a broad front and so ill-disciplined through foraging and pillage that they had to be rested for a fortnight in order to restore discipline and morale. The army had already suffered the equivalent of the casualties of two large battles and was harassed constantly by Cossacks and partisans before battling on to Smolensk. After brief resistance, the Russians abandoned Smolensk and retreated to Moscow, where the Tsar dismissed the 'foreigner' Barclay, a Lithuanian, and appointed as supreme commander the corpulent, one-eyed, wily and cautious Kutusov. Clausewitz, who had left the Prussian army for the Russian general staff, commented: 'the arrival of Kutusov revived confidence in the army. The evil genius of the foreigners was exorcised by a true native Russian ... and no one doubted that the battle would take place soon and halt the French offensive' (**191**, Ch. 5).

Urged on by the Tsar, the court and the nobility, Kutusov decided, rather against his better judgement, to stand and fight 115 kilometres west of Moscow, near the village of Borodino. A line of fortifications was hurriedly erected to protect his 120,000 men. As the *Grande Armée* marched east to give battle, Kutusov pushed his reserves too far forward, within range of the French artillery (**187**, Ch. 12). Napoleon had 130,000 men, nearly 25,000 fewer than at Smolensk, and 587 guns against the Russian 640. Napoleon himself was far below his best at Borodino. Not only did he receive news just before the battle of Marmont's defeat at Salamanca in Spain six weeks earlier, but the effects of a heavy cold left him uncharacteristically lethargic. Rejecting Davout's suggestion of a wide outflanking sweep to the south, he decided on a frontal assault against the Russian positions, largely because he lacked troops of the necessary quality for speedy manoeuvring (**190**, Ch. 2). The battle of Borodino lasted from six in the morning to four in the afternoon, when, with both sides exhausted, it petered out. This bloody battle of attrition cost the *Grande Armée* 28,000 men, including ten generals. Larrey, the chief surgeon, carried out 200 amputations in twenty-four hours. The Russians lost over 40,000, including Bagration. Hence Napoleon got the great pitched battle he sought, but not an overwhelming victory, as the Russians were able to retreat from Borodino in good order, a mere 700 being taken prisoner (**67**, Ch. 70). As the great Soviet historian Tarlé wrote in 1936: 'In the final accounting, Borodino proved a great moral triumph of the Russian people over the all-European dictator' (**184**, Ch. 5).

In Moscow, the Tsar's Council of War decided that the city could not effectively be defended, so Kutusov retreated south to protect the rich grainlands, taking with him most of the native population of Moscow. On 14 September Napoleon and his advance guard rode into Moscow, but two days after he had settled in the Kremlin fires were started by the Russian governor of the city in order to destroy markets and magazines. The huge conflagration consumed two-thirds of Moscow. Napoleon was in a perilous situation, for he found it difficult to prevent his men becoming an uncontrollable rabble as they looted and pillaged what was left of the city. His efforts to persuade the Tsar to make peace came to nothing, for even if Alexander had wished to respond he would have risked deposition, or even assassination, by doing so. Instead of negotiating, Alexander reinforced Kutusov's army. Meanwhile Cossacks and guerrillas harassed Napoleon's lines of communication, attacking convoys of sick and wounded and raiding supply trains. Stragglers had their throats cut by merciless peasants.

Napoleon eventually realized that he could not winter in Moscow without the *Grande Armée* starving to death. He resolved therefore to return to Germany by a route somewhat to the south of that which he had taken in the advance to Moscow. Here he hoped to find villages intact and have a chance of living off the land before reaching the supply depots he had left along the route from Smolensk to Vilna. On 19 October, the 120th day of the campaign, Moscow was evacuated, as many resident *émigrés* joined the French retreat. The Russians immediately attacked in a series of flanking assaults which pushed the *Grande Armée*, now 107,000 strong, plus thousands of civilians and waggons of loot from Moscow, northwards towards the Smolensk road. So the *Grande Armée* was forced to return to Smolensk by the same route on which it had advanced to Moscow, and was obliged to march past the field of Borodino, still strewn with the naked and mutilated corpses of French soldiers. Kutusov was perfectly content to keep prodding the *Grande Armée* to the west and off Russian soil, judging correctly that Napoleon would be unable to hold his Empire together after so colossal a failure.

The experiences of the *Grande Armée* in its retreat from Moscow have become a by-word for suffering. Men were already living off horseflesh, falling from sickness and being constantly attacked by

Russian marauders. Even before snow and intense cold appeared, the main section of the *Grande Armée* had shrunk to 55,000 men and 2,000 horses. The snow itself began to fall on 6 November, just before Smolensk was reached. After pausing for only five days – there being no food in the town and the Russian armies pressing on their flanks – Napoleon's forces set off west again. At this stage the Russians decided to destroy the French army, rather than allowing it to escape, by preventing it reaching and crossing the River Beresina. Two Russian armies reached the river before the French and demolished the bridges. Yet the *Grande Armée*, or at least the greater part of what was left of it, succeeded in getting across. Napoleon skilfully sneaked between the Russian armies and discovered a ford. Here General Eblé, chief engineer and commander of the pontoon-bridge building units, directed 300 sappers to work in freezing water amid ice floes. This heroic bridge-building effort saved the *Grande Armée*. Twice Eblé's *pontonniers* had to repair bridges under a Russian mortar barrage. When the bridges were finally fired to prevent a Russian pursuit, about 50,000 French had crossed, leaving 25,000, mostly civilians, behind. Thousands more had drowned trying to struggle across the freezing water. The *Armée* was no longer *grande* [**doc. 25**].

The suffering continued, as Cossacks attacked in temperatures of −17 centigrade. On 3 December, at Molodechno, Napoleon issued a bulletin describing the disasters of the retreat and blaming them on the weather. Two days later, he left the army and headed for Paris. He was deeply worried by news of the Malet Plot. Malet was a royalist conspirator imprisoned in 1806 and later moved to a mental hospital. From there he spread rumours that Napoleon had died in Russia. With the aid of accomplices, he escaped and announced that he had been entrusted with a provisional government. He even had Savery, the chief of police, arrested before the plot was rumbled by the commander of the Paris garrison and quashed. What alarmed Napoleon was that so many intelligent people had accepted that his regime was over and had ignored the claims of the Empress and the King of Rome (**125**). Napoleon also wished to reach Paris before news of the Russian *débâcle* spread through the courts of Europe. Murat, left in charge of the remnants of the *Grande Armée*, lost all control as the last vestiges of discipline vanished. When the Russians stormed Vilna, preventing the army resting there and forcing the abandonment of 24,000 sick and wounded, Murat's nerve cracked and he handed over command to the more capable Eugène before departing for his kingdom of

Naples. On 11 December, Berthier wrote: 'every human effort is lost; one can only resign oneself' (**191**, Ch. 10).

This was the end, although Ney fought a celebrated rearguard action. 'The bravest of the brave' was the last man off Russian soil on 14 December 1812. Only 25,000 of the original main army of 400,000 got back across the Niemen, plus 70,000 of the flanking armies. About 160,000 horses and a thousand guns had been lost. The first survivors reached Königsberg on 20 December; others filtered back to various assembly points in East Prussia, where native French troops now met a hostile population. Only 400 of the 8,000 Young Guard who had left Moscow survived; only 1,500 out of 24,000 Westphalians. There was little comfort in the fact that the Russians had lost 200,000 and that Kutusov arrived at the Niemen with only some 40,000 effective troops. As Murat was heard to say just before he left for Naples: *'nous sommes foutus'*.

14   Last-Ditch Battles 1813-14

No sooner had the shattered remnants of the *Grande Armée* crossed
the Niemen than General Yorck accepted a convention with the
Russians on behalf of the Prussian contingent. Yorck's decision was
crucial. With his 14,000 Prussians the French would have been
able to halt the exhausted Russians on the Niemen and the Pregel
and give Napoleon the chance to collect new armies in East Prussia
and Silesia. Instead the French had no choice but to withdraw to
central Germany, encouraging the Russians to cross their border
and continue the war in the west (**201**, Ch. 6). Under pressure
from Stein and vociferous patriot groups, the hesitant Frederick
William signed the Treaty of Kalisch with the Tsar in February
1813, in order to try to recover Prussian territory lost after Jena
and persuade the German princes to join in a war of liberation
(**202**). The 120,000 reserve troops of the *Landwehr* were now
mobilized, forcing Eugene's army to evacuate Berlin and withdraw
west of the Elbe as Prussia declared war on France.

Once Prussia and Russia had allied against Napoleon, Austria's
attitude became crucial. Although France and Austria were linked
dynastically, Schwarzenberg's withdrawal of his Austrian force
from the *Grande Armée* in December 1812 was an ominous sign.
During the early months of 1813 Metternich played a complex
double game, aiming to safeguard Austria's interests by removing
the French from central Europe, but without having them replaced
by another great power, certainly not the Russian colossus. Unlike
the British, Metternich would have been content to see Napoleon
remain on the throne of France (**206** Ch. 2). But Austria's price for
her neutrality was French acceptance of an enlarged Prussia and
the dismantling of the Grand Duchy of Warsaw and the Confederation of the Rhine. Although such terms provided a realistic basis
for peace, Napoleon regarded them as unacceptable. Even so,
Austria hesitated to join the allies until it became clear, after
further peace feelers, that Napoleon was not willing to make
concessions, other than the return of the Illyrian provinces to the
Emperor Francis.

Disillusion in France after the failure of the Russian campaign, and a waning in popular support for his regime, made Napoleon decide to fight rather than seek genuine peace terms [**doc. 26**]. His priority early in 1813 was to create a new army capable of taking on the Russians and Prussians. On paper he collected 500,000 men, but desertion, evasion and delays in mobilization meant that he only had half this number immediately available for a campaign in Germany. At the same time, a massive appeal for supplies and equipment was launched throughout France. What could not be replaced were the 10,000 horses lost in Russia. Lack of sufficient cavalry was to prove a constant and fatal liability during the approaching campaign, when the only skilled French cavalry force was still embroiled in Spain (**68**, Ch. 5; **31**, Ch. 14).

By April, Napoleon had collected 225,000 men at Mainz and planned to strike through Erfurt towards Leipzig, snatch a quick victory, and then push the allies back over the Elbe. At the end of the month he commenced his manoeuvre and on 2 May defeated Wittgenstein at Lützen, just outside Leipzig. Shortage of cavalry, however, prevented a rigorous pursuit and destruction of the allied army, although the victory did persuade Saxony to renew her alliance with France. Combining his army with Eugène's force, Napoleon now advanced with 120,000 troops against an allied army of 96,000 at Bautzen, 50 kilometres east of Dresden. Ney's army marched simultaneously from the north in order to take the allies in their rear. Once again a French victory was marred by the inability to conduct an effective pursuit (**67**, Ch. 77).

During the subsequent brief armistice Napoleon lost his numerical advantage as the net began to close around the French. His continued refusal to accept the Rhine frontier as the basis of a peace settlement stiffened the resolve of the allies. Castlereagh's diplomatic plenipotentiaries also exerted pressure on the European monarchs by offering substantial British subsidies in return for firm treaties of alliance against the French (**208**). Bernadotte, now Prince Royal of Sweden, was induced to abandon his war against Denmark and join the allies, in return for a British subsidy and a promise of British support in a campaign to capture Norway. Metternich was persuaded to lay aside his fears that the Tsar might make a separate bargain with the French and gain domination of Poland and Germany for Russia. On 11 August Austria at last joined the alliance against the French. It had always been the case that if the European great powers sank their differences and stuck together, Napoleon was finished. Hitherto he had always been able to knock at least one country out of any coalition against him, but this was now unlikely as Alexander and Frederick William undertook not to make a separate peace. The allies were encouraged by the obvious decline in French mobility and military effectiveness, as well as by news of Wellington's victory in Spain at the battle of Vitoria. At this stage it was largely a question of manpower. The allies could draw on at least 800,000 men, with ample reserves, against Napoleon's 700,000, which included a high proportion of raw recruits.

Napoleon's strategy now was to pivot on Dresden and the territory between the Elbe and the Oder with a force of 300,000, in an attempt to isolate and defeat separately Bernadotte's 120,000 Swedes and Pomeranians, Blücher's 95,000 Prussians, and Schwarzenberg's 240,000 Austrians. But the allies were careful to avoid battle with the main French army, and instead concentrated on less skilled subordinate forces before moving against Napoleon himself. In August 1813 the allies began to converge on Dresden, where a series of encounters led to heavy casualties on both sides. Napoleon himself got the better of Schwarzenberg, but Marshals Macdonald and Oudinot were beaten by the Prussians. This was enough to encourage the allies to arrange a concerted strategy and move in for the kill. The German princes, scenting blood, hastened to join the allies. As further Russian forces appeared, Napoleon was inexorably pushed back on Leipzig, his armies ravaged by battle losses, desertion and disease.

By October 1813 Napoleon was pinned in Leipzig with only 200,000 troops, facing Schwarzenberg's 203,000; while Blucher's 54,000 and Bernadotte's 85,000 were moving towards him. There was a fatal period of hesitation before the French set out to destroy Schwarzenberg's forces prior to the arrival on the field of the other two armies. Napoleon's failure to gain a decisive victory on the first day sentenced him to defeat. Two days later, the Saxons having defected, he was outnumbered three-to-two in both men and guns as he faced a combined force of 300,000. After a full day's bloody fighting he had to call a retreat. The 'Battle of the Nations' cost the French 38,000 casualties and 30,000 prisoners. The allies lost 54,000 killed and wounded, but they had wrested control of Germany from the French, who could only retreat rapidly to the Rhine, leaving 100,000 soldiers besieged in German fortresses (**67**, Ch. 80) The battle of Leipzig therefore marked a stunning defeat for the French. Decimated by typhus, they were now pushed back to the 'national frontiers' and to the defence of France itself. The only hope for Napoleon was that Austria, Prussia and Russia would quarrel over the future of Germany and Poland and undermine their own alliance. Napoleon's hope was Britain's fear. Intense British diplomatic activity at the allied courts, led by the young Earl of Aberdeen, resulted in a treaty whereby the allies agreed to continue the war until Europe was free of French control (**209**, Ch. 12).

With the allies resolved to continue the war, Napoleon was doomed. Many Frenchmen now began to believe that he was acting out of regard for his own intense egoism rather than in the interests of their country. Commercial confidence slumped; opposition arose in the Legislature, which objected to further tax increases and demanded civil and political liberties, as well as a peace settlement. Napoleon's response was to prorogue the Legislature. As he wrote to Savary: 'I want no tribunes of the people; let them not forget that I am the great tribune' (**31**, Ch. 14). Some of his chief subordinates now defected, most notably Murat, who pledged the Kingdom of Naples to the allied cause. Nevertheless, Napoleon insisted on fighting to the bitter end. Having suffered 400,000 casualties in 1813, with Wellington pinning down a force of 200,000 in Spain, the Emperor needed to raise yet another army for the 1814 campaign by every possible expedient, including the conscription of army pensioners and young teenagers. There was a good deal of resistance. In the Tarn department, for example, 1,028 deserted out of the 1,600 called up. Eventually about 120,000 men were scraped together to face an allied force of at least 350,000.

Napoleon's chief concern was to save Paris, the heart of his Empire. For a time he was successful, as the allies quarrelled over the peace terms to be imposed on France and failed to co-ordinate the movements of their armies. Napoleon's defensive campaign in 1814, fighting with his back to the wall and possessing only raw troops against overwhelming numbers, was a brilliant one [**doc. 30**]. He seemed to recover all his old nervous energy, powers of concentration and quick thinking, as his moves constantly caught his opponents off balance. With a mere 30,000 men he defeated Blücher's 50,000-strong Army of Silesia in three battles in February, although the Prussians were eventually rescued by their Russian allies. Turning on Schwarzenberg, Napoleon drove him back from the Seine, exposing the allies' strategic error in operating with separate armies (**67**, Pt xvi). Even at this stage Napoleon was unwilling to accept peace terms, and Castlereagh again played on the Continental allies' chronic shortage of cash by offering subsidies in exchange for a firm decision to overthrow 'General Bonaparte' [**doc. 29**]. Blücher and Schwarzenberg pressed forward again in March, but Napoleon moved his battalions swiftly eastwards and, in a dazzling series of manoeuvres reminiscent of Italy in 1796, placed his army behind the Russian and Austrian forces. In this way he hoped to deflect the allies from their march on Paris. When some of Napoleon's despatches were intercepted and shown to the Tsar, he ordered Blücher and Schwarzenberg to continue their relentless advance on the French capital, where Talleyrand and a number of Senators were among those prudently adjusting themselves to the prospect of a Bourbon restoration. The citizens of Paris made no attempt to rise against the invaders, resistance being confined to the frontier regions. Marmont, with a small force, offered token opposition on the heights of Montmartre before signing the capitulation of the city. When Napoleon arrived at Fontainebleau on 31 March 1814, the Tsar was already riding in triumph through Paris (**69**, Ch. 17).

At a conference with his remaining marshals, Napoleon was urged to abandon a hopeless struggle against overwhelming odds. In France itself there was a serious financial crisis and widespread war weariness. When Napoleon talked of yet another campaign, his marshals rebelled. Ney, Lefebvre and Moncey told him that the army would no longer follow him. The Senate and the Legislature had already voted for his deposition. Napoleon therefore had no choice but to abdicate in favour of his young son, the King of Rome, on 4 April. When this proved unacceptable to the allies, he abdicated unconditionally on 6 April. Five days later, after a good deal of discussion on what to do with him, the allies announced that Napoleon would be exiled to the island of Elba, off the Italian coast. After an unnerving journey through royalist mobs in Provence – who threw stones at the windows of his coach and at Orgon hanged and shot him in effigy – Napoleon reached Fréjus and embarked on HMS *Undaunted*. Before the end of the month Louis XVIII was restored to the throne of France by will of the allies and invitation of the French Senate. It appeared that, after twenty-two years, the Revolutionary and Napoleonic Wars were over.

Once the allies had decided to depose Napoleon, the restoration of the Bourbons was inevitable. Indeed, it had been stipulated by Britain and Russia ten years previously (**216**). What mattered was the form the restoration should take. The Charter of 1814, by which Louis XVIII regained the throne of his ancestors, established a constitutional monarchy on the English model. There was to be no indemnity or army of occupation. But the main emphasis of the first Treaty of Paris (30 May 1814) was on the future containment of France, now confined within the borders of 1792 which Napoleon had recently imperiously rejected. The French retained the conquests of Richelieu, Mazarin and Louis XIV, but lost most of those of the Revolution and Napoleon. The colonies lost to Britain during the 1790s were largely restored, except for Tobago, Mauritius and some other small islands. In annexes to the main treaty, however, France was deprived of most of the attributes of great-power status, being robbed of influence over her smaller neighbours and lacking frontiers which she could easily control.

France became ringed by a series of hostile buffer states. Austria regained control of northern Italy, adding Venetia to Lombardy, while the Kingdom of Piedmont was strengthened by the addition of Genoa, as well as being bound to Austria by a defence treaty. The southern Netherlands were united with Holland, and Britain agreed to finance the erection of barrier fortresses along the Franco-Dutch border. Swiss independence was guaranteed. In the Rhineland, traditionally an area of French influence, Prussia gained both territory and dominance. Thus the three frontiers which France's armies had regularly crossed during the eighteenth century were strengthened against future French aggression. When the French eventually realized the significance of the full settlement, they were filled with resentment, not so much at the loss of territory, but at France's exclusion from her traditional spheres of influence. Meanwhile, in accordance with Article 32 of the Peace of Paris, the European powers agreed to meet in general congress at Vienna in September 'to complete the provisions of the present treaty' and to draw up a general settlement for the Continent.

15 The Hundred Days

During his ten months on Elba, Napoleon passed the time reorganizing the administration and economy of the island, while keeping an eye on French and European developments through his agents on the Italian mainland (**210**). In France there was not only bitterness at the terms of the Treaty of Paris, but also widespread hostility to the restored Bourbon regime, which soon made itself unpopular by failing to abolish Napoleon's most recent tax increases, by retaining conscription and by organizing constant processions, military parades and ostentatious religious ceremonies. The majority of the Napoleonic army, angry at demobilization plans and the prospect of victimization, as well as the reduction in the status of the Imperial Guard, remained much more loyal to the former Emperor than most of his marshals. Thirty thousand officers were disgruntled at being put on half-pay. There were also rumours that the Bourbons intended to deprive the propertied classes of what they considered to be their essential gains from the French Revolution. Many of the middle classes and the majority of the peasantry became convinced that the Bourbons would restore the *biens nationaux* – land confiscated from the Church and the *émigrés* – to their pre-1789 owners.

Meanwhile at the Congress of Vienna the powers were already in dispute over arrangements for central and eastern Europe. Between November 1814 and January 1815 the chief issue was the future of Poland and Saxony. Metternich was fearful of Russian expansion into central Europe, much of which was already occupied by the Tsar's army, and of Prussian dominance of northern Germany. Russia tended to interpret the concept of the 'balance of power' in terms of her own expansion rather than as a state of equilibrium, and was determined to take the whole of Poland, including Prussia's Polish territories – for which Prussia could compensate herself with Saxony. But if Russia took almost all Poland, and Prussia the whole of Saxony, then Austria's strategic position would be seriously jeopardized. Conflict over the Polish-Saxon question involved clashes and conflicting secret alliances between the powers and gave Talleyrand the chance to side with Metternich and exert French influence on the settlement. In the event, Russia gained Poland and Prussia three-fifths of Saxony.

Discontent in France and disputes among the allies at Vienna were welcome news to Napoleon. Further incentives for him to make a bid to regain his empire were the fact that he was running short of cash on Elba – for the allies were slow to pay the annual 2,000,000 francs they had awarded him – and that he heard of tentative allied proposals to move him to the West Indies or St Helena. He was also stung by the allegations of cowardice which were still being made against him. Given what appeared to be a favourable combination of circumstances, Napoleon resolved on one last gamble. Sailing in February 1815 with some of his guard in his one warship, he landed in France near Antibes on 1 March. With a tiny force of 1,000 men and four guns, he staked everything on the unpopularity of the Bourbons outside strongly royalist areas and on the appeal of his name to French soldiers and peasants. Paradoxically, it was the workers and peasants, for whom he had done relatively little, who flocked to him, while the *notables*, the prime beneficiaries of his regime, tended to hold aloof and await events.

Avoiding hostile Provence, he travelled over the mountain route from Cannes. In Dauphiné he was welcomed by 2,000 peasants, carrying torches of blazing straw and shouting '*Vive l'Empereur*', strongly encouraged by loyal Bonapartist soldiers of the Grenoble garrison (**38**, Pt iv, Ch. 9). Marshall Ney, despatched to capture 'the usurper' and bring him to Paris 'in an iron cage', was won over by the charm of his old master at Auxerre. From Lyon to Paris, Napoleon's progress was a march of triumph. After Louis XVIII left for Ghent in an undignified hurry, the common people of Paris gave Napoleon a rousing reception. With characteristic opportunism, he promised a reformed constitution and the creation of genuinely liberal government. A surprised Benjamin Constant was summoned to the Tuileries and invited to draft an *Acte additionel*, amounting to a new liberal constitution (**108**, epilogue; **214**). Even Murat changed sides again and prepared to take his Kingdom of Naples to war with Austria in Italy. Fouché, Carnot and Lucien Bonaparte proved willing to join a new liberal administration in Paris. Yet the enthusiasm for Napoleon in France did not run as deep as his triumphal progress to the capital had indicated, for there were mass abstentions in a hastily-arranged plebiscite.

Napoleon hoped that, now he was *de facto* ruler of France again, he would be able to agree peace terms with Austria and Britain and split the 1814 coalition. But Metternich and the British, encouraged by the renegade Talleyrand, rejected Napoleon's peace overtures, declared him an outlaw and joined Prussia and Russia in a Seventh Coalition. Once the allies had refused to recognize him as ruler of France, Napoleon's only option was a quick military victory that would unite the country behind him. Once more he applied himself to raising an army, having many more veterans available than in 1813–14 because of returned garrison troops and prisoners of war. Nevertheless he was obliged to have recourse to conscription. He ended up with fewer than 300,000 men; a third of these being required to guard the frontiers and police royalist areas. He was also badly in need of top-flight commanders and hampered by the death of Berthier, his invaluable chief-of-staff. Strategically, it was again a matter of trying to defeat the allied armies separately. If he struck quickly, before the Russians and Austrians had time to cross France's eastern frontier, it might prove possible to catch Wellington's army of 100,000 and Blücher's 120,000 strong Prussian force while they were still dispersed, and then prevent them from uniting, giving him the chance to defeat them in turn.

He nearly succeeded. The stealthy massing of 120,000 French troops on the Belgian frontier took the allies by surprise, as Napoleon moved forward between the converging forces of Wellington and Blücher. But he was unable to execute his strategic plan. Ney delayed attacking Wellington, giving him time to secure reinforcements and seek a good defensive position. Blücher was duly repulsed at Ligny, but the French were unable to push the Prussians away to the east as planned. When Wellington decided to stand and fight on the ridge of Mont St Jean, there were 81,000 Prussians on their way to help him. At the final battle of Waterloo, Napoleon lacked the energy and decisiveness he had revealed during the 1814 campaign. Too much was left to the impetuous Ney, who insisted on mounting suicidal assaults on British fortified positions, where the French were cut down by the murderous musket-fire of the disciplined British lines (**68**, Ch. 5; **212**). Once the Prussians began to join Wellington in the early evening, the French were doomed. Even the Imperial Guard, which had never failed since its formation eleven years earlier, fled in confusion before the British cavalry. Wellington, whose line had come perilously close to breaking in several places, owed everything to Blücher keeping his word and honourably supporting his ally (**213**, Ch. 3; **67**, Pt xvii).

In Paris the disillusioned Senate and Legislature, now anxious to be rid of Napoleon, called out the National Guard to prevent any attempt at dissolution of the chambers. Only one or two ministers were prepared to contemplate proclaiming the King of Rome as Napoleon II at a time when Wellington and Blücher were advancing on Paris, with Louis XVIII and his Bourbon court following 'in the baggage train of the allies'. Lacking support in the capital, Napoleon abdicated a second time, before travelling on to Rochefort. He now sought asylum with the British, embarking voluntarily on HMS *Bellerophon*, sent by the Admiralty to prevent his escape to the United States. He had ambitions of settling down as an English country gentleman, as his brother Lucien had been for some years. But the British government refused to entertain the idea of having so potent a symbol of the French Revolution on their soil. In any case, the allies had entrusted the British with the task of confining Napoleon in a place of no escape (**215**).

It was decided to send 'Boney' and a small personal entourage, plus a large British guard, to the rocky south Atlantic island of St Helena, 1,600 kilometres from the African coast. Here he lived until his death in 1821, when he was just short of fifty-two years old, writing his memoirs, conducting a feud with the severe British governor, Hudson Lowe, and having his conversations and interpretations of past events recorded for posterity. The exact nature of his final illness has never satisfactorily been diagnosed, but it was probably cancer of the stomach. The British insisted that his body stay on St Helena, but in 1840 gave permission for his remains to be taken to France, where they were reinterred with much ceremony in *Les Invalides* in Paris. A hundred years later, the body of his legitimate son, King of Rome and Duke of Reichstat, who died in 1832, was moved from Vienna, on the orders of Adolf Hitler, to lie beside that of his father.

Part Four: Assessment

16 Legend and Reality

One obstacle in the way of historians trying to reach a balanced assessment of the career of Napoleon is the power of the Napoleonic legend, which has persisted from the time of the Consulate to the present day, inspiring novelists, poets and playwrights from Byron and Hugo to André Malraux, musicians from Beethoven to Prokoviev, painters in the nineteenth century and film-makers in the twentieth (**222**). The cult of the heroic grandeur of Napoleon was even an important ingredient in the Gaullism of the 1950s and 1960s.

The chief author of the Napoleonic myth was, of course, Napoleon himself. From 1797 onwards he used press propaganda, bulletins, parades and censorship to extol his own image (**111**, Ch. 2). Painters like Gros, David and Ingres were recruited to provide definitive images of the hero-superman. Even foreigners were impressed. Hegel, watching the Emperor's entry into Berlin in 1806, claimed that he had seen 'the world spirit'. In exile on St Helena, Napoleon devoted most of his time to embellishing his own legend and responding to writers like Germaine de Staël, Chateaubriand and Benjamin Constant who were already portraying him as 'the Corsican Ogre', more akin to Attila the Hun and Genghis Khan than Caesar or Charlemagne (**126**). Napoleon's conversations with the Comte de Las Cases, published in 1823 as *Mémoriale de Saint Hélène*, amounted to a skilful attempt at reinterpreting his career and depicting himself as the guardian of liberty and equality, the promoter of peaceful economic co-operation, the heir and defender of the principles of the French Revolution; a ruler whose autocracy was an unavoidable necessity in order to defend France against the machinations of Britain and the duplicity of the Continental monarchs, with their anxiety to preserve feudalism and inequality (**31**, Ch. 17). He claimed that his campaigns were either purely defensive, in order to conserve the Revolutionary heritage against those who wished to erase the gains of 1789 and restore the Bourbons, or were intended to liberate and unify fragmented and oppressed peoples. Although Napoleon admitted mishandling Spain from

1808, he nevertheless posed as the patron of nationalism and progress against paternalist feudal princes: a genuine 'people's Emperor' standing firm against obscurantism and reaction.

There was sufficient truth in some of these claims for them to be swallowed indiscriminately by many of the younger generation after 1815. Relatively few, other than ardent royalists, were prepared to accept Chateaubriand's argument that the Emperor had always been an essentially destructive force, despising the vast majority of his fellow men and suppressing all genuinely free opinion. Those who had been too young to fight in Napoleon's campaigns, and felt that they had missed their rightful share of glory, adventure and excitement, helped to sustain a cult of Napoleon which was already flourishing in popular songs and verses. This cult provided a hero for what Lamartine called 'a bored generation', by emphasizing the glory and the conquest, the reckless daring and dynamism, while ignoring the deaths, disablement and loss of all meaningful political liberty (**221**, Ch. 2; **220**, Pt i, Ch. 3). Romantic poets and writers like Alfred de Vigny, Alfred de Musset, Victor Hugo and Honoré de Balzac joined in the nostalgia for life before 1815, whose excitement contrasted with existence under the stiff and reactionary Bourbons, or the dull 'bourgeois' Orléans monarchy after 1830. In his novels, Stendhal portrayed idealistic and Romantic young men, eager to model themselves on Napoleon in order to make an impression on society. Outside France, poets like Heine, Manzoni and Pushkin played their part in exalting Napoleon as a heroic Christ-figure, crucified by the allies (**222**, Ch. 5).

When the biographers of Napoleon and historians of the Consulate and Empire began to appear after 1820, they tended to divide between admirers and detractors. Attitudes were invariably coloured by the political affiliations of the writer. Before 1848 Napoleon was idealized by those on the left who formed the opposition to the Bourbons and Orléanists. Right-wing historians and biographers, often fervently anti-British French nationalists opposed to democratic principles, glorified Napoleon very much along the lines of the *Mémoriale de Saint Hélène*. After 1871 they extolled the warrior Napoleon as a means of berating France for her military failure against Prussia and of criticizing the politicians of the Third Republic for neglecting the army and avoiding a war of revenge to regain Alsace-Lorraine and 'the blue line of the Vosges' (**55**, intro.).

Bonapartist political propagandists, especially after 1830 – when the revolution of that year brought back into power many Napoleonic generals and officials excluded in 1815 – exalted Napoleon's genius and advocated his methods as a means of reconciling authority and democracy and dispensing with discredited parliaments. Unlike royalism, which had an equal claim to stand for the maintenance of order and security of property, Bonapartism in nineteenth-century France aspired, through its interpretation of Napoleon I's career, to preserve the work of the Revolution by affirming the principles of equality, careers open to talent and the abolition of social privileges (**224**, Ch. 18). During the 1920s, Napoleon's detractors on the left again came to the fore, reviving the '*légende noire*' of Napoleon as a man of blood, responsible for setting France on the road that led to the slaughter of Verdun in 1916. Right-wing literary historians, usually based on the *Académie française*, riposted against the university historians by reviving the peace-loving, progressive Napoleon, whose quasi-fascist authoritarianism was necessary to prevent the dissolution of the social order.

In his classic *Napoleon: For and Against* (1944), the Dutch historian Pieter Geyl magisterially reviewed the differing interpretations of Napoleon's career put forward by French historians, in what he termed 'an argument without end'. Jean Tulard, in his masterly survey of the Napoleonic legend in 1977, portrayed Napoleon as the first in a line of 'saviours' supported by the French bourgeoisie when it felt its interests vitally threatened. After Napoleon, the role was filled by Cavaignac, Louis Napoleon, Thiers, Clemenceau, Pétain and De Gaulle, each of whom was expected to solve a major crisis, such as *coup d'état*, revolution, defeat in war or loss of empire (**222**, intro.). Views of Napoleon will continue to differ. As Geyl wrote: 'truth, though for God it may be one, assumes many shapes to men' (**220**, Pt i). Napoleon can be seen as the dynamic leader of Revolutionary forces unleashed in 1789, with his outlook and actions largely determined by those inexorable pressures. This is very much the view taken by Tolstoy in his great novel *War and Peace* (1869). Napoleon can also be depicted as an unprincipled adventurer, whose genius owes more to propaganda than to deeds, as in Barnett's 1978 biography. Attention may be focussed on his constructive achievements, especially the programmes of legal and administrative reform. It can equally be concentrated on the tyranny, exploitation and bloodshed. During the Napoleonic Wars, 5.5 per cent of the French population (equivalent to about 23 per cent of men of military age) became casualties, compared with 3.4 per cent for the admittedly much shorter First World War.

Napoleon may be admired as a key figure in the development of the modern state, with its enormous power over the lives of individual citizens and the fate of the local community (**55**, Ch. 3). It is equally possible to see him as the forerunner of twentieth-century totalitarian dictatorship, lacking only the technology of film and radio and massive bureaucracy to rank with Stalin, Hitler and their subsequent imitators. Writing from an extreme liberal individualist point of view, Richard Cobb has characterized the Consulate and Empire as 'France's most appalling regime' (**122**, Pt ii, Ch. 3). There has been much debate on how far Napoleon's career and policies were based on the principles of 1789, if not those of 1792. He both fulfilled and distorted the legacy of the French Revolution, jettisoning popular political principles like the sovereignty of the people, but preserving equality before the law and the material gains of the bourgeoisie and more prosperous peasantry. It is certainly difficult to see the 'heir of the Revolution' in a ruler who, for example, gagged the press and restored slavery in France's colonies. On the other hand, Napleon stood by the principle of religious toleration; his attitude towards the Jews putting many subsequent European regimes to shame. Other matters for dispute include the question of how far Napoleon was 'the last of the enlightened despots'; how far he was a 'good European', as he claimed on St Helena; or how far he was a dictator with an insatiable lust for conquest. From the point of view of the conquered territories, was the abolition of feudalism and the introduction of legal and administrative reforms sufficient to outweigh the financial exactions, the burden of conscription and the operation of the Continental System to serve the economic interests of France? Even Napoleon's military genius may be called into question, if his errors at Marengo, his performance at Aspern-Essling and his gigantic blunders in invading Spain in 1808 and Russia in 1812 are carefully assessed.

It is evident that each writer, and indeed each reader, constructs his own Napoleon from the mass of evidence available. More books have been written on Napoleonic France and Europe than days have elapsed since Napoleon's death in 1821. The shelves of libraries are weighed down by biographies, monographs and detailed analyses of policy. His military career, government and administration, personality, sex life, even his very anatomy, have been subjected to minute scrutiny. Books continue to pour from the presses, containing every possible argument, including allegations that he was slowly changing into a woman, or was poisoned by arsenic contained in the wallpaper at Longwood, his residence on St Helena.

In the interpretation of Napoleon's career and its impact on France and Europe, a good deal depends, not only on the predilections of author and reader, but also on what particular aspects and what particular chronological stages of that career are emphasized. Few can fail to admire the dynamic young Napoleon in Italy in 1796–7 and his courage in grasping power when other talented generals like Moreau and Joubert hesitated. Even fewer would attempt to defend the murder of the Duc D'Enghien or the slaughter of 2,000 disarmed Turkish prisoners in Syria. Many would perhaps concur with David Chandler when he applies to Napoleon the judgement of Clarendon on Cromwell: 'a great bad man' (**68**).

For Frenchmen, Napoleon will always remain fascinating as their countryman who made most impact on the world. Nationalists and Romantics see his monument in the *Arc de Triomphe* or the flags of *Les Invalides*. Marxists, on the other hand, view him as little more than the compliant tool of the confident and expanding bourgeoisie – the servant of emerging capitalism (**33**). Others value Napoleon for the laws and institutions which he bequeathed to France and which still persist in modified form. Non-Frenchmen are understandably more immune to the effects of the Napoleonic legend, and therefore tend to highlight the darker aspects of his regime and the cynical and calculating side of his personality. It is certainly easy to exaggerate Napoleon's influence on both France and Europe. Arguably, France changed less between 1800 and 1815 then between 1785 and 1800. Napoleon's regime did not last long enough to achieve real stability. The social élites were never fully integrated into his system; the Church soon recovered its Ultramontane spirit and was never completely loyal. Economic life changed only very slowly (**52**). Liberalism in Europe owed more to the Revolution than to Napoleon. What does remain certain is that the debate on the career and impact of Napoleon Bonaparte will continue for the foreseeable future, not least in France itself; for, as H.A.L. Fisher wrote seventy years ago: 'Never was so brilliant a fugue upon the twin themes of patriotism and glory addressed to the multitude of any country' (**21**, Ch. 10).

Part Five: Documents

document 1
The new art of war

Clausewitz served in the Prussian army from 1792. He fought in the Jena-Auerstädt campaign and, attached to the Russian army, in the 1812 war in Russia. His Vom Kriege, *published a year after his death in 1831, raised the study of war to a new level.*

Thus War [before 1789] in reality became a regular game in which Time and Chance shuffled the cards; but in its signification it was only diplomacy somewhat intensified, a more vigorous way of negotiating, in which battles and sieges were substituted for diplomatic notes. To obtain some moderate advantage in order to make use of it in negotiations for peace was the aim even of the most ambitious ... Plundering and devastating the enemy's country ... were no longer in accordance with the spirit of the age. They were justly looked upon as unnecessary barbarity, which might easily induce reprisals ... War, therefore, confined itself more and more, both as regards means and end, to the Army itself ...

Thus matters stood when the French Revolution broke out; Austria and Prussia tried their diplomatic Art of War; this very soon proved insufficient. Whilst, according to the usual way of seeing things, all hopes were placed on a very limited military force in 1793, such a force as no one had any conception of made its appearance. War had again suddenly become an affair of the people and that of a people numbering thirty millions, every one of whom regarded himself as a citizen of the State ... By this participation of the people in the War instead of a Cabinet and an Army, a whole Nation with its natural weight came into the scale. Henceforward, the means available – the efforts which might be called forth – had no longer any definite limits; the energy with which the war itself might be conducted had no longer any counterpoise, and consequently the danger to the adversary had risen to the extreme ... this was perfected by the hand of Buonaparte, this military power, based on the strength of the whole nation, marched over Europe, smashing everything in pieces so surely and certainly, that where it only encountered the old-fashioned Armies, the result was not doubtful for a moment. A reaction, however, awoke in due time. In Spain the war became of itself an affair of the people ...

C. von Clausewitz, *On War*, ed. Col. F.N. Maude and trans. Col. J.J. Graham, Routledge and Kegan Paul, 1908; Penguin ed. 1968, pp. 382-85

document 2
Napoleon's personality

Caulaincourt was one of Napoleon's closest intimates, whose memoirs are a major source for the Russian campaign, as well as for personal details of the Emperor.

When he so wished, there could be a power of persuasion and fascination in his voice, his expression, his very manner, giving him an advantage over his interlocutor as great as the superiority and flexibility of his mind. Never was there a man more fascinating when he chose to be ... Woe to him who admitted a single modification, for the adroit interlocutor led him from concession to concession to the end he had in view, casting up a previous concession against you if you defended yourself, and assuming that it consequently implied the point you refused to concede. No woman was ever more artful than he in making you want, or agree to, his own desire when he thought it was to his interest to persuade you, or merely wanted to do so. These reflections call to my mind what he once said on a similar occasion, which explains better than any other phrase could have done the price he was ready to pay for success: 'When I need anyone,' he said, 'I don't make too fine a point about it; I would kiss his ...'.

The Emperor needed much sleep, but he could sleep when he wanted to, by day as well as by night ... On a campaign he was awakened for everything. Even the Prince of Neuchâtel [Berthier], who received and despatched and knew his Majesty's plans, decided nothing ... The Emperor occupied himself with the most minute details. He wanted everything to bear the imprint of his genius. He would send for me to receive his orders for headquarters, for the orderly officers, for his staff officers, for the letters, for the couriers, postal service etc. The commanding officers of the guard; the controller of the army commissariat; Larrey, the excellent surgeon-general; all were summoned at least once a day. Nothing escaped his solicitude. Indeed, his foresight might well be called by the name of solicitude, for no detail seemed too humble to receive his attention ... he had an astonishing memory for localities. The topography of a country seemed to be modelled in relief in his head. Never did any man combine such a memory with a more creative genius. He seemed to extract men, horses and guns from the very bowels of the earth. The distinctive numbers of his regiments, his army service companies, his baggage battalions, were all classified in his brain most marvellously. His memory sufficed for everything. He knew where each one was, when it started, when it should arrive at its destination ...

But his creative genius had no knowledge of conserving its forces. Always improvising, in a few days he would consume, exhaust and disorganize by the rapidity of his marches, the whole of what his genius had created. If a thirty-days' campaign did not produce the results of a year's fighting, the greater part of his calculations were upset by the losses he suffered, for everything was done so rapidly and unexpectedly, the chiefs under him had so little experience, showed so little care and were, in addition, so spoiled by former successes, that everything was disorganized, wasted and thrown away ... The prompt results of the Italian and Austrian campaigns and the resources those countries offered to the invader spoiled everyone, down to the less important commanders, for more rigorous warfare. The habit of victory cost us dear when we got to Russia and even dearer when we were in retreat; the glorious habit of marching ever forward made us veritable schoolboys when it came to retreating.

J. Hanoteau, (ed.) *Memoirs of General de Caulaincourt, Duke of Vicenza 1812–13*, trans. H. Miles, Cassell, 1935, pp. 599-601

document 3

The morale of the troops

French success in the Italian campaign of 1796–7 owed much to the high morale of the Army of Italy, partly a creation of army newspapers published in Milan, distributed free to the troops and circulated in France. These papers concentrated on instilling loyalty to Napoleon throughout the French army.

He moves at the speed of light and strikes like a thunderbolt. He is everywhere at once and misses nothing ... If one examines his domestic life, one finds a man who happily divests himself of all grandeur when with his family; he has the constant air of a man preoccupied with some great scheme, which frequently interrupts his meals and his sleep. He says with simple dignity to those whom he respects: 'I have seen kings at my feet; I could have amassed fifty millions in my coffers; I could easily have claimed to be someone other than what I am; but I am a citizen of France, I am the leading general of *La Grande Nation*; I know that posterity will do me justice'.

Le Courrier de l'armée d'Italie, 23 October 1796; cited in J. Tulard, *Napoléon*, Paris, Fayard, 1977, p. 84

Long live General Bonaparte!

document 4

The wife of General Junot knew Napoleon from his youth. Here she describes his reception in Paris in 1797 as a conquering hero after the first Italian campaign. The law of the maximum was a system of price controls imposed during the French Revolution.

However great Napoleon's vanity, it must have been well satisfied, for, as I have said, all classes united to welcome him on his return home. The people cried: 'Long live General Bonaparte!', 'Long live the conqueror of Italy!', 'Long live the peace-maker of Campo Formio!' The bougeoisie said: 'May God preserve him, for the sake of our glory and for delivering us from the law of the maximum and the Directory!' The upper class, now ungagged and released from their chains, ran with enthusiasm towards a young man who in a year had passed from the battle of Montenotte to the Treaty of Leoben, from victory to victory. Since then it has become possible to see his faults, even serious ones, but during that epoch he was seen as a pure and mighty colossus of glory. All the authorities provided magnificent *fêtes* for him; the Directory appeared in all its ludicrous pomp, including cloaks and plumed hats, which made the union of state power from five parts look somewhat ridiculous. While the *fêtes* were splendid in themselves, they possessed the added charm of celebrating the restoration to us of what we thought we had lost. Money began to circulate again, and the result of it all was that everyone was content.

Laure, Duchesse d'Abrantès, *Mémoires*, Paris, Chez Ladvocat, 1831, Vol. ii, Ch. 7, pp. 123-34

The *coup d'état* of Brumaire, November 1799

In a conversation with Madame de Rémusat in 1803, Napoleon recalled his tactics at the time of Brumaire.

I was very careful. It was one of the periods of my life when I acted with the soundest judgement. I saw the Abbé Sieyès and promised him that his wordy Constitution would be put into effect. I received the leading Jacobin and Bourbon agents. I listened to advice from everyone, but gave advice only in the interests of my own plans. I hid myself from the people, because I knew that when the moment came, curiosity to see me would bring them running after me. Everyone was caught in my nets and when I became head of the state there was not a party in France that did not build some special hope on my success.

Paul de Rémusat (ed.), *Memoirs of Madame de Rémusat 1802–1808*, trans. C. Hooey and J. Lillie, Sampson, Low, 1881, Vol. i, p. 100

The indifference of the Paris Crowd

The sans culottes *had been savagely repressed after the risings of 1795 and there was no further insurrection before 1830, although Napoleon distrusted the common people and kept the capital under close police surveillance.*

The situation in the Faubourg Antoine is not such as to cause any anxiety. Admittedly, discontented elements try every day to stir up agitation, but the vast majority of the inhabitants, although discontented at the lack of work and stagnation of trade, refuses to join in any kind of popular movement and is firmly against taking the least part in such movements.

Police report, 16 May 1800, Archives de la Préfecture de Police, Paris, Series Aa

document 7

Popular enthusiasm for Napoleon

Lamartine, the Romantic poet and liberal politician, was born at Mâcon in 1790, the son of a petty noble army officer. Milly was the village where the Lamartine country residence was situated.

The first example of political enthusiasm which I remember, and which made an impression on me, took place in a village square adjoining the courtyard of our residence. The enthusiasm was that of a young man named Janin, who was rather better educated than his neighbours, and who taught the children of the parish to read. One day, he emerged from an old shack, which served as a school, to the sound of a clarinet and the beat of a drum. Having gathered round him the boys and girls of Milly, he showed them the pictures of great men which the book-hawker at his side was selling. 'Here', he said to them, 'is the the battle of the Pyramids in Egypt, which General Bonaparte won. He is the small, thin, dark man who is darting about with his long sabre in his hand, in front of those piles of trimmed stones which are called pyramids'. The book-hawker spent the afternoon selling copies of this manifestation of national glory, which Janin explained to the wine-growers. His enthusiasm spread through the district. Thus it was that I felt the first sensations of *la gloire*. A charger, a plume, a mighty sabre, became symbolic. These people remained soldiers for a long time afterwards, perhaps for ever. On winter evenings, in the stables, they talked about the sales of this book-pedlar, and Janin was constantly being called back to their houses to decipher the texts of those splendid and truthful images.

Alphonse de Lamartine, *Mémoires inédites*, Paris, Plon, 1870, p. 31

document 8

The triumph of Marengo

Thibaudeau, at this time prefect at Bordeaux, had been a supporter of the coup d'état *of Brumaire and noted how victory at Marengo consolidated Napoleon's position and prestige in France.*

The victory at Marengo decided the fate of Italy and proved a happy omen for France. The Cisalpine Republic was re-established, the Ligurian Republic liberated, the annexation of Piedmont secretly prepared. The First Consul and the Catholic Church formed an alliance at Milan. The Church sang his triumphs and treated him as a sovereign. The victory anthems and the mood of triumphant joy spread to Paris, to Bordeaux and throughout the Republic. A campaign so short, so brilliant and so decisive had never previously been witnessed. Covered in laurels, the First Consul swiftly travelled across Italy, laid the foundation stone of the restoration of the *place de Bellecour* at Lyon, and then returned to Paris, able to say, with justice, like Caesar: *veni, vidi, vici.* He arrived on the 13 Messidor [2 July 1800] at two o'clock, with a slight wound from an accident to his carriage. The whole population flowed into the courtyard and garden of the Tuileries palace. Everyone's face expressed a joy which had not been seen for a long time.

Mémoires de A.–C. Thibaudeau 1799–1815, Paris, Plon, 1913, pp. 26–7

document 9

Napoleon's unorthodox religious beliefs

Sometimes Napoleon claimed to be a devout Catholic, but these recorded conversations with Bertrand on St Helena offer a more realistic view of his actual beliefs.

12 June 1816: the Emperor then spoke about the New Testament: 'Faith guarantees us the existence of Jesus Christ, but historical proof is lacking. Josephus is the sole evidence and even then only through marginal details which some people regard as later additions. He says only that Jesus Christ appeared and was crucified. But history is full of men who have been executed as criminals and to whom you could apply what has been said about Jesus Christ. The gospel writers offer no facts that can be substantiated, and in this respect, some people say, write with considerable skill. The gospel writers are rarely content with a sound moral and few facts ... Mohammed, on the other hand, was a conqueror and a sovereign, and his existence is incontestable ...'

Général Bertrand, *Cahiers de Sainte-Hélène 1816–1819*, ed. P. Fleuriot de Langle, Paris, Albin Michel, 1959, pp. 64–5

document 10
England's greed and ambitions

Written by Napoleon himself, this extract from a long editorial diatribe in the official government newspaper, Le Moniteur, *depicted the renewal of war in 1803 and the end of the Peace of Amiens as entirely the fault of the British.*

If France had possessed ambitious schemes and ideas of aggrandizement, would she not have kept all Italy under her direct influence? Would she not have annexed the Batavian Republic, Switzerland and Portugal? Instead of these easy acquisitions, she wisely offers to limit her territory and power, and she accepts the loss of the huge territory of San Domingo as well as of the large sums of money and the armies which have been sent to recover that colony. She makes every sacrifice so that peace may continue ... For the sake of indulging her malignant and all too powerful passions, England disturbs the peace of the world, wantonly violates the rights of nations, tramples on the most solemn treaties, and breaks her pledged faith – that ancient and eternal faith which even savage hordes acknowledge and religiously respect.

One sole obstacle stands in the way of her policies and her ambitions – victorious, moderate, prosperous France; her vigorous and enlightened government; her illustrious and magnanimous leader. These are the targets of England's delirious envy, of her constant attacks, of her implacable hatred, of her diplomatic intrigues, of her maritime conspiracies, and of the official denunciations of France to her Parliament and subjects. But Europe is watching; France is arming. History writes: Rome destroyed Carthage!

Le Moniteur, May 1803

document 11
Police repression

Fouché was a key figure in Napoleon's system of government as Minister of Police 1799–1802 and 1804–10. Napoleon himself was a firm believer in an efficient police network and here reveals his unwillingness to tolerate opposition from the Church.

To M. Fouché, Minister of the General Police. Paris, 14 February 1806.

I see in your bulletin of 13 February, article Deux-Sèvres, that these young ladies, La Rochejaquelin, Gibot, and others, have given refuge to some dissident priests. Issue orders for them to be sent away in exile to towns in Dauphiné, like Vienne, and take diligent steps to arrest these priests.
Napoléon.

L. Lecestre (ed.), *Lettres Inédites de Napoléon Ier*, Vol. i, Paris, Plon, 1897, p. 65

Police and public

document 12

The police spent much of its time in Paris monitoring public opinion and issuing daily bulletins on price movements and fluctuations on the stock market. The coincidence of bad news from Spain and the Malet conspiracy caused official anxiety.

Paris: Today everyone is very concerned about Spain and what is going on there. As usual, it is all exaggerated. The Ministry of Police has taken measures to squash false rumours. People are no longer complaining about the high price of coffee and sugar; many people go without them and do not complain. The capital enjoys the greatest tranquillity. Events have shown that all the anxieties to which we have sought to respond are only really calumnies against this city. The agitators are punished by the public contempt in which they are held ...

Ministry of the General Police, Bulletin of 23 June 1808, printed in A. Aulard (ed.), *Paris sous le premier Empire*, Vol. iii, Paris, Cerf, 1923, p. 652

Police and the problem of desertion

document 13

Fouché's police were constantly concerned with the question of bands of deserters, often organizing sweeps to round them up.

Bulletin of Saturday, 3 June 1809. Western region. Measures taken by the Ministry. In a previous issue of the Police Bulletin on the troubles which are disturbing the west, it has been established that the basic elements in these outbreaks consist of a considerable mass of defaulters and deserters which the prefects, while providing their numerical contingents of conscripts, have allowed to accumulate, year by year, in their departments. But at the same time, the duration and persistence of these agitations reveal that they are not simply agitations against conscription, but also the work of English agents and of discontented elements in these regions. It is hoped that the surrender, either spontaneous or forced, of a large proportion of conscript deserters, who form part of the gangs, will throw some light on the formation and operation of these bands of men, on those who incite them and those who support them, on their motives and their resources ...

E. D'Hauterive (ed.), *La Police secrète du premier Empire: Bulletins quotidiens addressés par Fouché à l'Empereur*, Vol. v, Paris, Clavreuil, 1964, pp. 67–8

document 14

French rule in Naples

Napoleon made it clear to the rulers of the satellite kingdoms that the interests of France should have priority.

Paris 8 March 1806
To Prince Joseph
My Dear Brother, I see that you promise, in one of your proclamations, not to impose any war taxation; and that you forbid our soldiers to demand full board from their hosts. In my opinion you are adopting measures that are too narrowly conceived. You do not win people to your side by cajoling them, and it is not by measures like these that you will gain the means of providing your army with its rightful recompense. Levy a contribution of thirty millions from the Kingdom of Naples; pay your army generously, re-equip your cavalry; have shoes and uniforms manufactured; all this can only be done with money. So far as I am concerned, it would be too ridiculous if the conquest of Naples did not bring comfort and well-being to my army. It is unthinkable that you should confine yourself within such limits. Rest your case, if you wish, on my orders ... do not promise to preserve either fiefs or exemptions which have been allowed from the tax system, for it is necessary to establish in Naples taxes on land and on legal documents, as in France; and, finally, if you must grant fiefs, it is necessary to give them to Frenchmen who uphold the Crown. It has not been

reported to me that you have had any *lazzaroni* shot, but I am aware of their stiletto attacks. If you do not make yourself feared from the beginning, you are bound to get trouble. Imposing taxation will not have the effect you imagine; everyone expects it and finds it perfectly natural ... Your proclamations to the people of Naples do not make it clear enough who is master. You will gain nothing by too many caresses. Both the people of Italy and people in general will, if they detect they have no master over them, turn to rebellion and mutiny.

Correspondance de Napoléon Ier, publiée par ordre de l'Empereur Napoléon III, Vol. xii, Paris, Plon-Dumaire, 1863, no. 9944, pp. 165–6

document 15

The benefits of French rule

The breath-taking first sentence reveals Napoleon's attitude to the 'independence' of his brother 'monarchs'.

Fontainebleau, 15 November 1807
To Jérôme Bonaparte, King of Westphalia
My Dear Brother, You will find enclosed the constitution of your kingdom. This constitution contains the conditions on which I renounce all my rights of conquest and all the claims I have acquired over your kingdom. You must observe it faithfully. The happiness of your people is important to me, not only because of the influence it can have on both your reputation and mine, but also from the point of view of the whole European system. Refuse to listen to those who tell you that your subjects, accustomed to servitude, will greet the benefits you offer to them with ingratitude. They are more enlightened in the Kingdom of Westphalia than some would have you believe; and your throne will only become truly established with the confidence and affection of the people. What the peoples of Germany impatiently desire is that men of talent, who lack noble rank, will have an equal claim to your favour and to government employment; they also demand that all kinds of servitude and intermediate links between the sovereign and the lowest class of the people be entirely abolished. The benefits of the *Code Napoléon*, public trials, the introduction of juries, will be the distinctive features of your rule ... It is necessary for your subjects to enjoy a degree of liberty, equality and prosperity hitherto unknown among the peoples of Germany; and that

your liberal government produces, one way or another, changes which will be most salutary for the Confederation of the Rhine and for the strength of your monarchy. Such a method of government will prove a more powerful barrier separating you from Prussia than the Elbe, the fortresses and the protection of France. What people would wish to return to the arbitrary government of Prussia when they have tasted the benefits of wise and liberal administration? The peoples of Germany, as well as those of France, Italy and Spain, desire equality and demand liberal ideas. I have been managing the affairs of Europe long enough to be convinced that the burden imposed by the privileged classes is contrary to the wishes of general opinion. Be a constitutional king.

Correspondance, Vol. xvi (1864), no. 13361, pp. 166–7

document 16

A scolding for Louis Bonaparte

After becoming King of Holland, Louis showed a marked tendency to identify with the interest of his Dutch subjects, rather than with those of France and his brother.

Trianon, 21 December 1809
To Louis Napoleon, King of Holland
I have received your Majesty's letter, which asks me to declare my intentions concerning Holland. I will do so frankly.

When your Majesty assumed the throne of Holland, one section of the Dutch nation desired union with France. Studying its history enhanced the esteem in which I hold this noble nation, and led me to wish that it preserve its name and its independence. I myself drew up its constitution, which was to furnish the basis of your Majesty's throne, upon which I placed you. I hoped that, developing in close proximity, it would possess that affection for France which the French nation has the right to expect of its children, and even more so of its princes. I hoped that, raised in my political principles, you would feel that Holland, which has been conquered by my subjects, only owes its independence to their generosity; that Holland, lacking allies and an army, could be, and would deserve to be, conquered the day it set itself in opposition to France; that it ought never to separate its policies from my own; that in the final analysis Holland is bound to me by treaties. I hoped also that, in placing on the throne of Holland a prince of my own blood, I had found the *mezzo termine* which reconciled the interests of the two states and united them in common concerns and mutual hatred for England; and I was very proud of having given Holland what best suited her ... But it did not take me long to realize that I was under a vain illusion. My hopes have been deceived. Your Majesty, in ascending the throne of Holland, has forgotten that he is French, and has used all his powers of reason, while tormenting his delicate conscience, to persuade himself that he is Dutch. Those Dutchmen who incline to France have been scorned and persecuted. Frenchmen, both officers and other ranks, have been hounded and discredited, and I have been mortified to see in Holland, under a prince of my own family, the name of Frenchman exposed to humiliation. However, the honour of the name of France is so close to my heart, while maintained by the bayonets of my soldiers, that neither in Holland nor elsewhere can such a slur be cast with impunity ... And what have the Dutch to complain about? Were they not conquered by our arms? Do they not owe their independence to the generosity of my subjects? Ought they not to be grateful to France for opening its waterways and its customs barriers to their commerce? Grateful to France, which conquered Holland in order to protect it, and which, right up to this very moment, has employed its power only to consolidate Dutch independence? What, therefore, could justify your Majesty's conduct, insulting to the French nation and offensive to me personally? ... Your Majesty is deluded about my character, being misled by my goodwill and friendly feelings. You have violated all the treaties you made with me; you have disarmed your fleets, discharged your crews, run down your armies, so that Holland finds herself without armed forces on land or sea; as if commodities, merchants and clerks were able to constitute power ...

Your Majesty has done more: profiting during the moment when I was embarrassed elsewhere on the Continent to permit the renewal of relations between Holland and England, violating the rules of the Blockade – the sole efficient means of nullifying England's power ... Your Majesty will find in me a brother, provided that I find in you a Frenchman; but if you forget the ties which attach you to our common country, then you will not be unpleasantly surprised if I forget the natural affinity between us ... I have sufficient grievances against Holland to declare war on her ...

Lettres inédites de Napoléon Ier, Vol. i, pp. 382–5

document 17

Smuggling in Alsace

This report by the sub-prefect of Altkirch to the prefect of the Haut-Rhin in
September 1805 is typical of many throughout the French empire which reveal
the widespread evasion of French economic regulations and the Blockade.

It is unfortunately only too true that smuggling is undertaken on a
frightening scale from the point of view of the interests of our
factories and workshops and of the public treasury ... Public
opinion designates many individuals, even government officials,
who must be engaged in it or who are protecting it; one can safely
say that men of both high and low rank are involved; the latter are
caught up in it by the lure of gain, which the leading figures
provide by paying handsomely for the contraband peddling which
usually goes on at night.

Archives Départementales du Haut-Rhin, Colmar, P295. French
text cited in G. Ellis, *Napoleon's Continental Blockade*, Oxford University
sity Press, 1981, p. 205

document 18

The Continental System: France first!

The Continental System was designed not only as a weapon against Britain,
but also as an instrument of French economic domination of European
markets. In this letter Napoleon was reinforcing his demand that French
products be permitted free entry into Italy. Eugène Beauharnais was his step-
son by Josephine's first marriage.

Saint-Cloud, 23 August 1810
To Eugène Napoléon, Viceroy of Italy, at Monza
My Dear Son, I have received your letter of 14 August. The silks of
the kingdom of Italy seem to go entirely to England, since silks are
not manufactured in Germany. Obviously I wish to modify this
trade route to the profit of French manufactures, for without it my
silk products, which are a principal staple of French trade, will
suffer considerable losses. I cannot accept the observations you
make. My motto is: France first. You must never lose sight of the
fact that, if English commerce triumphs on the seas, that is because
the English dominate the oceans; it is therefore logical that, since
France is superior on land, she should make her trade dominant

there; otherwise all is lost. Would it not be better for Italy to come to the aid of France in such circumstances, rather than find herself covered with customs-posts? For it would be very unwise not to recognize that Italy is independent only with the goodwill of France; that this independence has been gained by French blood and French victories, and that Italy must clearly not abuse it; that it would therefore be very injudicious to try to decide whether or not France ought to obtain significant commercial advantages ... Italy must not make calculations independent of the need to assure the prosperity of France; she must combine French interests with her own; above all, she must avoid giving France a motive for the annexation of Italy, for if France decided to do so, who could stop her? Therefore you should take for your motto: France first.

Correspondance, Vol. xxi (1867), no. 16824, pp. 60–1

document 19
The horrors of war

This horrific account of the aftermath of the battle of Eylau, fought in a snowstorm on 8 February 1807, was written by a surgeon in the French forces and provides a corrective to the celebrated Romantic painting of the battlefield by Baron Gros.

Never were so many corpses crammed into so confined a space. The snow was everywhere stained with blood; the snow which had already fallen, and that which continued to fall, began to hide the cadavers [corpses] from the aggrieved eyes of passers-by. Where there were clumps of fir trees, behind which the Russians had fought, corpses were piled in heaps. Thousands of muskets, caps and breastplates were scattered along the road, or in the fields. On the side of a hill, the reverse slope of which had been chosen by the Russians as a good defensive position, there were mounds of a hundred bloody corpses. Horses, wounded and crippled but still alive, waited until hunger would cause them to fall, in their turn, on to the piles of dead. Hardly had we crossed one battlefield, than we came upon another: all of them strewn with bodies.

Percy, *Mémoires*, Paris, 1904; cited in J. Tulard, *Napoléon*, Fayard, Paris, 1977, pp. 192–3

document 20
Optimism in 1810

The failures in Spain had done nothing to dent Napoleon's confidence in 1810.
This harangue was delivered to a deputation from the electoral college of the
Dordogne.

My ally, the Emperor of Russia, and I have done everything we
could to bring peace to the world, but we have not been able to
succeed. The King of England, grown old in his hatred of France,
wants war. His condition [madness] prevents him from realizing
the evil to the world and from calculating the results for his family.
However, the war will come to an end; and then we shall be
greater, stronger and more powerful than we have ever been. The
French Empire has the vitality of youth; it can only grow and
consolidate itself. That of my enemies is in its latter years; everything presages its decline. Each year that they delay the peace of
the world will only increase my power.

Journal de Paris, 8 February 1810, cited and translated in I. Collins,
Napoleon and his Parliaments, Arnold, 1979, p. 92

document 21
The Austrian marriage 1810

Thibaudeau, prefect at Marseilles from 1803 to 1815, was a staunch
Republican who cared little for the establishment of the Empire and even less
for the marriage between Napoleon and Marie-Louise, which made 'the heir
of the Revolution' a nephew of Louis XVI. Thibaudeau, Fouché and
Cambacérès were all former members of the Convention and regicides.

I was on the point of leaving Paris when the marriage contract
between Napoleon and Marie-Louise was signed. My wife very
much desired to be present at the Imperial wedding, which promised to be an interesting spectacle. I asked for, and obtained, an
extension of my official leave. Invited as a Councillor of State, I
was present at the civil marriage ceremony in the gallery of the
Palace of Saint-Cloud. I found myself next to Marshal Masséna ...
He was even less enthusiastic than I was about this marriage with
an Austrian. We exchanged pleasantries during the ceremony,

which was as chilly and gloomy as a funeral. I felt I had had enough. I did not plan to go and be crammed into the gallery of the Louvre for the religious ceremony the following day. My wife went, but I preferred to mingle freely on the streets. I waited in the *Champs Elysées* to watch the arrival of the Imperial procession, which was really magnificent. I then circulated among the crowd, which had been attracted only out of simple curiosity and which displayed neither enthusiasm nor joy. Among high state officials, I was not the only one to remain cool about this marriage, which created so many anxieties. As far as men of the Revolution were concerned, neither instinct nor reason led them to see any good in it. Fouché explained this to me himself. In the attitude of Cambacérès, despite his characteristic caution, I detected both embarrassment and discomfort.

Mémoires de A.–C. Thibaudeau 1799–1815, Paris, Plon, 1913, pp. 278–9

An unpopular war

document 22

Macdonald was the only marshal created on the field of battle, at Wagram in 1809. An attack of gout enabled him to leave his unpalatable task in Spain in September 1811.

After the Emperor's marriage he appointed me Commander-in-Chief of the Army of Catalonia and Governor-General of the Principality·in April 1810. I had a very strong objection to the manner in which the war was carried on in Spain; my objection had its root in the dishonesty – or what in high places is called policy – which caused the invasion of the country; however the noble and courageous resistance of its inhabitants triumphed over our efforts and our arms. I obeyed, nevertheless, and started. I led a very active life, that was as odious as it was exhausting. The enemy were ubiquitous, and yet I could find them nowhere, though I travelled through the length and breadth of the province.

C. Rousset (ed.), *Recollections of Marshal Macdonald, Duke of Tarentum*, trans. S. L. Simeon, Richard Bentley, 1893, p. 186

Reform of the Prussian Army

Defeat at Jena and Auerstädt led not only to the adoption of new tactics by the Prussian Army, but also to new regulations on officer selection, signed by King Frederick William on 6 August 1808.

From now on, a claim to officer rank shall in peacetime be warranted only by knowledge and education, in time of war by exceptional bravery and quickness of perception. From the whole nation therefore, all individuals who possess these qualities can lay title to the highest positions of honour in the army. All social preference which has hitherto existed ceases completely in the army, and everyone, without regard to his social background, has equal duties and equal rights.

E. von Frauenholz, *Das Heerwesen des XIX. Jahrhunderts*, Munich, 1941, pp. 121–3, cited and trans. in P. Paret, *Yorck and the Era of Prussian Reform 1807–1815*, Princeton University Press, 1966, p. 133

The Russian campaign

Captain Fantin des Odoards, a veteran of Ulm, Austerlitz, Friedland and Spain, and now with the Grenadiers of the Old Guard, wrote this entry in his journal on 1 March 1812, just before leaving Paris for Metz to embark on the Russian campaign.

It is going to begin, this new campaign which will greatly increase the glory of France. The formidable preparations are made, and our eagles will soon take wing towards countries of which our fathers scarcely knew the names ... The Russian army is not to be despised, no doubt: a large population attacked at home is not easily subjugated. Spain proves that, but what is there that the great Napoleon cannot achieve? Besides, we cannot avoid going to visit the favourite city of the Peter who deserved the name 'Great'. St Petersburg will see us within its walls just as Vienna, Berlin, Rome, Madrid, and so many other capitals have done. Then we shall see.

In these circumstances I share the thoughts of the whole army.

It has never shown itself more impatient to run after fresh triumphs. Its august leader has so accustomed it to fatigue, danger and glory that a state of repose has become hateful. With such men we can conquer the world.

L.–F. Fantin des Odoards, *Journal du Général Fantin des Odoards. Etapes d'un officier de la Grande Armée 1800–1830*, Paris, 1895; cited and trans. in A. Brett-James, *1812*, Macmillan, 1966, p. 11

document 25

The horrors of the retreat from Moscow

At least 25,000 were left behind at the crossing of the Beresina, including many women, children, and French émigrés in Moscow who had returned with the Grande Armée. *Rochechouart, a French émigré lieutenant in the Russian Imperial Guard, arrived at the place where 50,000 of the French army had crossed on 30 November 1812.*

Nothing in the world more saddening, more distressing! One saw heaped bodies of men, women and even children; soldiers of all arms, all nations, choked by the fugitives or hit by Russian grapeshot; horses, carriages, guns, ammunition waggons, abandoned carts. One cannot imagine a more terrifying sight than the appearance of the two broken bridges, and the river frozen right to the bottom. Immense riches lay scattered on this shore of death. Peasants and Cossacks prowled around these piles of dead, removing whatever was most valuable ... On the bridge I saw an unfortunate woman sitting; her legs dangled outside the bridge and were caught in the ice. For twenty-four hours she had been clasping a frozen child to her breast. She begged me to save the child, unaware that she was holding out a corpse to me! She herself was unable to die, despite her sufferings, but a Cossack did her this service by firing a pistol in her ear so as to put an end to her appalling agony.

Both sides of the road were piled with dead in all positions, or with men dying of cold, hunger, exhaustion, their uniforms in tatters, and beseeching us to take them prisoner. They listed all their attainments, and we were assailed with cries of: 'Monsieur, take me along with you. I can cook, or I am a valet, or I am a barber. For the love of God give me a piece of bread and a strip of cloth to cover myself with'. However much we might have wished to help, unfortunately we could do nothing.

Général Comte de Rochechouart, *Souvenirs sur la Révolution, l'Empire et la Restauration*, Paris, 1889, pp. 187–90; cited and trans. in A. Brett-James, *1812*, Macmillan, 1966, pp. 260–1

document 26

Disillusion in Paris

Colonel de Fezensac, aide-de-camp to Marshal Berthier, noted the forebodings in the capital after the failure of the Russian campaign.

The short time I spent in Paris that winter left me with sad and lasting memories. I found my family, my friends and society in general terror-stricken. The famous 29th Bulletin of 17 December had informed France abruptly that the *Grande Armée* had been destroyed. The Emperor was invincible no longer. While we were dying in Russia, another army was perishing in Spain, and in Paris an obscure conspirator had tried to seize power. The campaign of 1813 was about to open, but in what circumstances! The defection of Prussia was no longer in doubt; the Austrian alliance was at the least very shaky; and the exhaustion of France increased in proportion as the list of her enemies grew longer. The stories told by officers who had survived the retreat contributed to intensify people's fears. Paris, used as she had been to songs of victory during the previous fifteen years, was learning day by day and with pained surprise the details of some fresh public or private calamity. The amusements of the carnival stopped. Everyone stayed at home, preoccupied with present misfortunes and anxiety for the future.

M. le Duc de Fezensac, *Souvenirs militaires de 1804 à 1814*, Paris, 1863, pp. 355–6

document 27

German nationalism

Fichte, a former Jacobin, delivered his Addresses to the German Nation *as a series of lectures in French-occupied Berlin during the winter of 1807–08.*

It is only by means of the common characteristic of being German that we can avert the downfall of our nation, which is threatened by its fusion with foreign peoples, and win back again an individuality that is self-supporting and quite incapable of any dependence on others ... we alone must help ourselves if help is to come to us ... By means of the new education we want to mould the Germans into a corporate body. It is the general aim of these addresses to bring courage and hope to the suffering, to proclaim joy in the midst of deep sorrow, to lead us gently and softly through the hour of deep affliction ... The German, if only he makes use of all his advantages, can always be superior to the foreigner ... only the German really has a people and is entitled to count as one; he alone is capable of real and rational love for his nation.

Johann Gottlieb Fichte, *Addresses to the German Nation*, ed. G.A. Kelly, Harper and Row, 1968, pp. 98–100

document 28

Conscription in 1813

Cambacérès, Second Consul and then Arch-Chancellor of the Empire, was Napoleon's chief executive in France. The drafts of 1,397 of his letters to Napoleon, discovered in Cuba in the 1950s, are a major source for the operation of Imperial government.

5 November 1813. Sire, the Council which has been charged by Your Majesty to advise on the means of raising a new levy of 140,000 men and of finding a supply of 60–80,000, met today for the second time. We listened to General d'Hastrel, who assured us that, according to the latest reports he had received, the levy will reach 140,000 as Your Majesty wishes. So results are already good.

As for the 60–80,000 extra men, it had been acknowledged that we can no longer think in terms of unmarried men, since the last available conscript in this category has already been called up. There is little evidence that we can count on the willingness to volunteer of married men, for most of them have only contracted marriage in order not to join up, and the price of substitutes is so high that such a measure as purchasing replacements would be impracticable, unless we recruit married men. General d'Hastrel proposed launching a call-up of the classes of 1806 and 1807, and of married men without children from the classes of 1806–1810. These proposals were discussed and appeared to raise certain problems, as well as having uncertain results. So the Council came round to the view of the Minister of the Interior, which was to call up 100,000 men from the National Guard, with no exemption for married men. In order to render this measure rather less rigorous, the Council decided to authorize prefects to grant small pensions to the families of those who would cause much suffering by their absence. In taking this view, the Council acknowledged the hard law of necessity.

Cambacérès: Lettres inédites à Napoléon 1802–1814, ed. J. Tulard, Paris, Editions Klincksieck, 1972–3, Vol ii, pp. 1108–9

document 29

Closing the ring

During the campaign in France in 1814, Castlereagh was instrumental in holding the allies together and in persuading Russia and Austria to sink their differences in the Treaty of Chaumont, signed in March.

I feel it more than ever necessary to conjure you and your colleagues at headquarters not to suffer yourselves to descend from the substance of your peace, You owe it, such as you have announced it, to the enemy, to yourselves, and to *Europe*, and you will now more than ever make a fatal sacrifice both of moral and political impression, if under the pressure of those slight reverses which are incident to war, and some embarrassments in your council which I should hope are at an end, the great edifice of peace was suffered to be disfigured in its proportions. Recollect what your military position is ... If we act with *military* and *political* prudence, how can France resist a just peace demanded by 600,000 warriors. Let her, if she dare, and the day you can declare the fact to the French nation, rest assured Bonaparte is subdued ... There can be in good sense but one interest among the Powers; namely, to end nobly the great work they have conducted so near to its close.

Castlereagh to Metternich, 18 February 1814, cited in C. K. Webster, *The Foreign Policy of Castlereagh 1812–15*, G. Bell, 1931, pp. 216–17

Napoleon and Marie-Louise

In his Italian campaign of 1796–97, Napoleon comforted himself by writing regularly to Josephine. During the 1813–14 campaign he sent frequent letters to Marie-Louise, though he tended to address her as one might a young child. The engraving he mentions sold thousands of copies and adorned many a cottage wall.

My dear, You have sent me a very lovely sweet-dish, with the portrait of the King of Rome at prayer. I desire you to have it engraved, with this motto: '*I pray to God that he will preserve my Father and France*'. This little reproduction is so interesting that it will give pleasure to everyone. I am sending to you Mortemart, a captain in the Ordnance, with 10 flags taken from the Russians, Prussians and Austrians. My health is good. The Emperors of Russia and Austria and the King of Prussia are at Pont, the home of *Madam* [Pont-sur-Seine, the estate of Napoleon's mother]. They are going to march precipitately on Troye. My troops have entered Nogent and Sens.

Give a kiss to my son, look after yourself, and never doubt all my love.

Nap   Montreau, 20 February 1814; 9 in the morning.

Lettres inédites de Napoléon Ier à Marie-Louise: Ecrites de 1810 à 1814, ed. Louis Madelin, Editions des Bibliothèques Nationales de France, Paris, 1935, letter 264

Bibliography

At least 60,000 books and articles have been published on Napoleon and Napoleonic Europe. The following bibliography is therefore highly selective, with some bias towards books in English. Fuller bibliographies may be found in: Villat, L. *Napoléon*, Paris, Bibliothèque Nationale, 1936; Godechot, J. *L'Europe et l'Amérique à l'époque napoléonienne*, Paris, P.U.F., 1967, and **38** below.

For the general background to the period, see:

1 Bruun, G. *Europe and the French Imperium 1799–1814*, New York, Harper, 1938.
2 Ford, F. L. *Europe 1780–1830*, Longman, 1970.
3 Hampson, N. *The First European Revolution 1776–1815*, Thames and Hudson, 1979. Superbly illustrated.
4 Crawley, C. W. (ed.) *The New Cambridge Modern History*, Vol. ix, *War and Peace in An Age of Upheaval 1793–1830*, Cambridge University Press, 1965.
5 Roberts, J. M. *The French Revolution*, Oxford University Press, 1978.

Among the enormous range of primary sources, the following may be consulted:

6 *Correspondance de Napoléon Ier*, 32 vols, Paris, Plon-Dumaire, 1855–70.
7 Thompson, J. M. (ed.) *Napoleon's Letters*, Dent, 1954. A selection.
8 Lecestre, L. (ed.) *Lettres inédites de Napoléon Ier*, Paris, Plon, 1897.
9 Hauterive, E. de 'Lettres de jeunesse de Bonaparte', *La Revue des Deux Mondes*, Dec. 1931.
10 Howard, J. E. (ed.) *Letters and Documents of Napoleon 1769–1802*, Cresset press, 1961.
11 Herold, J. C. (ed.) *The Mind of Napoleon*, New York, Columbia University Press, 1955.

In major libraries may be consulted the correspondence (disguised as *Mémoires*) of Joseph Bonaparte (1856–58), Jérôme Bonaparte (1861–66) and Eugène de Beauharnais (1858–60), as well as Louis Bonaparte, *Documents historiques et réflexions sur le gouvernement de la Hollande* (1820).

Essential for the operation of Napoleonic government are:

12 Bertrand, B. (ed.) *Talleyrand: lettres à Napoléon 1800–1809*, Paris, Plon, 1889.

13 Tulard, J. (ed.) *Cambacérès: lettres inédites à Napoléon*, 2 vols, Paris, Klincksieck, 1974.

14 Tulard, J. *Bibliographie critique des mémoires sur le Consulat et l'Empire*, Geneva, Droz, 1971, lists 794 volumes of memoirs, with critical comments. Among the more important are:

15 Chair, S. de (ed.) *Napoleon's Memoirs*, Faber and Faber, 1948.

16 Chaptal, Comte de *Mes souvenirs sur Napoléon*, Paris, Plon, 1893.

17 Ségur, Philippe-Paul de *An aide-de-camp of Napoleon 1800–1812*, Hutchinson, 1895.

18 Thibaudeau, A–C. *Mémoires*, Paris, Plon, 1913.

19 Hanoteau, J. (ed.) *Memoirs of General de Caulaincourt, Duke of Vicenza*, Cassell, 1935.

Among the large number of biographies of Napoleon are:

20 Holland Rose, J. *The Life of Napoleon I*, G. Bell, 1902.

21 Fisher, H. A. L. *Napoleon*, Oxford University Press, 1912. A concise classic.

22 Ludwig, E. *Napoleon* (1924), Arden Library, 1979.

23 Bainville, J. *Napoleon* (1932), Kennikot Press, 1970. The *Action française* view.

24 Kircheisen, F. M. *Napoleon* (1931), Arno Books, 1972.

25 Lefebvre, G. *Napoléon*, Paris, Presses Universitaires de France, 1935. The sixth edition of 1965 has been translated into two volumes, Routledge and Kegan Paul, 1969. A magisterial 'life and times'.

26 Thiry, J. *Napoléon Bonaparte*, 28 vols, Paris, Berger-Levrault, 1938–75.

27 Butterfield, H. *Napoleon* (1939), Macmillan, 1962.

28 Godechot, J. *Napoléon*, Paris, Presses Universitaires de France, 1969.

29 Thompson, J. M., *Napoleon Bonaparte: His Rise and Fall*,

Blackwell, 1952.
30 Markham, F. M. H. *Napoleon and the Awakening of Europe*, English Universities Press, 1954.
31 Markham, F. M. H. *Napoleon*, Weidenfeld and Nicholson, 1963. Still the best biography in English. See also his essay in 4 above.
32 Dowd, D. L. *Napoleon: Was He the Heir of the Revolution?* New York, Krieger, 1957.
33 Tarlé, E. *Napoléon*, Foreign Languages Press, Moscow, 1937.
34 Zagli, C. *Napoleone e l'Europa*, Naples, Cymba, 1969. Mainly on foreign policy.
35 Cronin, V. *Napoleon*, Collins, 1971; Penguin, 1973. Very favourable to Napoleon.
36 Jones, R. B. *Napoleon: Man and Myth*, Hodder and Stoughton, 1977.
37 Barnett, C. *Bonaparte*, Allen and Unwin, 1978. A colourful exercise in denigration.
38 Tulard, J. *Napoléon ou le Mythe du Sauveur*, Paris, Fayard, 1977. The best single volume survey in any language, by the successor to Madelin and Lefebvre as the *doyen* of Napoleonic studies. Includes a perceptive *critique* of recent research.

For the Napoleonic clan, see:
39 Knapton, E. J. *Josephine*, Cambridge, Mass., Harvard University Press, 1964.
40 Nabonne, B. *Pauline Bonaparte*, Paris, Hachette, 1964.
41 Connelly, O. *The Gentle Bonaparte: a biography of Joseph*, New York, Macmillan, 1968.
42 Nabonne, B. *Le roi philosophe* [Joseph], Paris, Hachette, 1949.
43 Bertault, J. *Le roi Jérôme*, Paris, Flammarion, 1954.
44 Oman, Carola *Napoleon's Viceroy: Eugène de Beauharnais*, Collins, 1966.
45 Bernhardy, F. *Eugène de Beauharnais*, Paris, Armand Colin, 1973.
46 Martinet, A. *Jérôme Napoleon: roi de Westphalie*, Paris, Payot, 1902.
47 Raillecourt, L. de *Louis Bonaparte*, Paris, Peyronnet, 1963.
48 Lacour-Gayet, G. *Talleyrand*, 4 vols, Paris, Payot, 1928–34.
49 Cooper, Duff *Talleyrand*, Jonathan Cape, 1932.
50 Thiry, J. *Cambacérès*, Paris, Berger-Levrault, 1934.
51 Papillard, F. *Cambacérès*, Paris, Hachette, 1961.

Bibliography

Among recent one-volume surveys of the Napoleonic period are:
52 Bergeron, L. *L'Episode Napoléonien: Aspects intérieurs 1799–1815*, Paris, Seuil, 1972; translated by R. R Palmer as *France Under Napoleon*, Princeton, N. J., Princeton University Press, 1982. Especially good on social and economic affairs.
53 Lovie, J. et Palluel-Guillard, A. *L'Episode Napoléonien: Aspects extérieurs*, Paris, Seuil, 1972.
54 Soboul, A. *Le Directoire et le Consulat*, 'Que Sais-je?', Paris, Presses Universitaires de France, 1967. A Marxist view.
55 Soboul, A. *Le Premier Empire*, 'Que Sais-je?', Paris, Presses Universitaires de France, 1973.

For Napoleon's early career see:
56 Colin, Commandant J. *L'Education militaire de Napoléon*, Paris, Chapelot, 1901. A classic.
57 Wilkinson, S. *The Rise of General Bonaparte*, Oxford University Press, 1930.
58 Mirtil, M. *Napoléon d'Ajaccio*, Paris, Flammarion, 1947.
59 Thiry, J. *Les années de jeunesse de Napoléon*, Paris, Berger-Levrault, 1975.
60 Chuquet, A. *La jeunesse de Napoléon*, 3 vols, Paris, Armand Colin, 1897–98.
61 Masson, F. *Napoléon chez lui*, new ed., Paris, Tallandier, 1977.
62 Parker, H. T. 'The Formation of Napoleon's Personality', *French Historical Studies*, vii, 1971.
63 Holland Rose, J. *The Personality of Napoleon*, G. Bell, 1912.
64 Tourtier-Bonazza, C. de (ed.) *Napoléon: lettres d'amour a Joséphine*, Paris, Fayard, 1982.
65 Madelin, L. (ed.) *Lettres inédites de Napoléon Ier à Marie-Louise 1810–14*, Paris, Bibliothèque Nationale, 1935.

For the changes in warfare during the French revolution see:
66 *Annales historiques de la Révolution francaise*, 210, 1972: special number on warfare.

For Napoleon's contribution to the art of war, see **56** and **57** above, and:
67 Chandler, D. *The Campaigns of Napoleon*, Weidenfeld and Nicholson, 1967. Definitive.
68 Chandler, D. *Napoleon*, Weidenfeld and Nicholson, 1973. Chapter 6 summarizes **67** above for those who lack the stamina for over a thousand pages.

69 Marshall-Cornwall, Gen. Sir James *Napoleon as Military Commander*, Batsford, 1967.
70 Quimby, R. S. *The Background of Napoleonic Warfare*, new ed., Seeley Service, 1977.
71 Howard, M. *War in European History*, Oxford University Press, 1976. A masterpiece of concision.
72 Best, G. *War and Society in Revolutionary Europe*, Fontana, 1982. Very stimulating.
73 Colin, Commandant J. *La campagne de 1796–97*, Paris, Chapelot, 1898.

For Napoleon's marshals, generals, soldiers and sailors, see **53** above, and:
74 Chardigny, L. *Les maréchaux de Napoléon*, Paris, Tallendier, 1979.
75 Macdonald, A. G. *Napoleon and his Marshals*, Macmillan, 1934.
76 Marshall-Cornwall, Gen. Sir James *Marshal Masséna*, Oxford University Press, 1965.
77 Gallager, J. *The Iron Marshal* [Davout], Evanston, Illinois University Press, 1976.
78 Watson, S. J. *By Command of the Emperor: Marshal Berthier*, Allen Lane, 1957.
79 Six, Général G. *Les Généraux de la Révolution et de l'Empire*, Paris, Payot, 1947.
80 Lucas-Dubreton, J. *Soldats de Napoléon*, Paris, Tallendier, 1977.
81 Richardson, R. C. *Larrey: Surgeon to Napoleon's Imperial Guard*, John Murray, 1974.
82 Choury, M. *Les grognards et Napoléon*, Paris, Perrin, 1968.
83 Thomazi, A. *Les marins de Napoléon*, new ed., Paris, Tallendier, 1977.
84 Glover, R. 'The French Fleet 1807–14', *Journal of Modern History*, 39, 1967.

For Napoleon's Italian campaigns and his policy in Italy, see **57** and **67** above, and:
85 Ferrero, G. *The Gamble: Buonaparte in Italy 1796–97*, G. Bell, 1961.
86 Thiry, J. *Bonaparte en Italie*, Paris, Berger-Levrault, 1973.
87 Roberts, J. M. 'Italy', in **4** above.
88 Chandler, D. 'Adjusting the Record: Napoleon and Marengo', *History Today*, 17, 1967.

89 Rodger, A. B. *The War of the Second Coalition 1798–1801*, Oxford University Press, 1964.

90 Ragsdale, H. 'Russian influence at Lunéville', *French Historical Studies*, 5, 1968.

91 Godechot, J. 'L'Armée d'Italie de 1796 à 1799', *Cahiers de la Révolution française*, 1936.

92 Ragsdale, H. *Detente in the Napoleonic Era: Bonaparte and the Russians*, Lawrence, Kansas, Regents Press, 1980.

For Egypt and the Middle East, see:

93 Herold, J. C. *Bonaparte in Egypt*, Hamish Hamilton, 1962.

94 Charles-Roux, F. *Bonaparte: Governor of Egypt*, Methuen, 1937.

95 Thiry, J. *Bonaparte en Egypte*, Paris, Berger-Levrault, 1973.

96 Puryear, V. J. *Napoleon and the Dardanelles*, Berkeley, University of California Press.

97 Crosland, M. *The Society of Arcueil*, Heinemann, 1967. A study of leading French scientists.

On the Directory and the *coup d'état* of Brumaire, see:

98 Lefebvre, G. *The Directory* (1937), Routledge and Kegan Paul, 1965.

99 Woronoff, G. *La république bourgeoise*, Paris, Seuil, 1972.

100 Lyons, M. *France Under the Directory*, Cambridge University Press, 1975.

101 Woloch, I. *Jacobin Legacy: the Democratic Movement under the Directory*, Princeton, Princeton University Press, 1970.

102 Goodspeed, D. J. *Bayonets at St Cloud*, Hart Davis, 1965.

103 Suratteau, J-R. 'Le Directoire après des travaux récents', *Annales historiques de la Révolution francaise*, 224, 1976.

104 Lynn, L., Causley, D. and Hanson, P. 'The Failure of the Liberal Republic in France 1795–1799: the road to Brumaire', *Journal of Modern History*, 51, 1979.

105 Church, C. H. 'In Search of the Directory', in Bosher, J. F. (ed.) *French Government and Society 1500–1850*, Athlone Press, 1973.

106 *La France à l'époque napoléonienne*, Paris, Armand Colin, 1970, contains 38 essays on all aspects of Napoleonic France.

107 Godechot, J. *Les institutions de la France sous la Révolution et l'Empire*, 2 vols, Paris, Presses Universitaires de France, 1951. See also Godechot's essay in **106** above.

108 Collins, I. *Napoleon and his Parliaments*, Edward Arnold, 1979.

109 Canabis, A. *La Presse sous le Consulat et l'Empire*, Paris, Presses Universitaires de France, 1975.

110 Matthews, J. J. 'Napoleon's Military Bulletins', *Journal of Modern History*, 22, 1950.

111 Holtman, R. B. *Napoleonic Propaganda*, Baton Rouge, Louisiana University Press, 1950.

112 Whitcomb, D. 'Napoleon's Prefects', *American Historical Review*, 79, 1974.

113 Durand, C. 'Conseils privés, conseils des ministres, conseils d'administration', *Revue d'histoire moderne*, 1970.

For the Church and the Concordat, see:
114 Godel, J. 'L'église selon Napoléon', *Revue d'histoire moderne*, 1970.

115 Dansette, A. *Histoire religieuse de la France contemporaine: L'Eglise catholique*, one vol. ed., Paris, Flammarion, 1965.

116 Macleod, H. *Religion and the People of Western Europe 1789–1870*, Oxford University Press, 1981, Ch. 5.

117 Hales, E. E. Y. *Napoleon and the Pope*, Eyre and Spottiswoode, 1962.

118 Walsh, J. 'Religion', in **4** above.

119 Masson, F. *Le Sacre et le Couronnement de Napoléon*, new ed., Paris, Tallendier, 1979.

For the police, opposition to the regime and resistance to conscription, see **109** above, and:
120 Arnold, E. E. *Fouché, Napoleon and the General Police*, New York, University Press of America, 1979.

121 Hauterive, E. de *Napoléon et sa police*, Paris, Flammarion, 1945.

122 Cobb, R. C. *The Police and the People 1789–1820*, Oxford University Press, 1970.

123 Madelin, L. *Fouché*, 2 vols, Paris, Plon, 1901.

124 Tulard, J. 'Quelques aspects du brigandage sous l'Empire', *Revue de l'Institut Napoléon*, 98, 1966. Argues that highwaymen and robber bands were never suppressed.

125 Villefosse, L. et Bouissounouse J. *L'Opposition à Napoléon*, Paris, Flammarion, 1969. On the Malet conspiracy.

126 Tulard, J. *L'Anti-Napoléon*, Paris, Julillard, 1964. Edited documents.

127 Kitchin, J. *La Décade 1794–1807: un journal 'philosophique'*, Paris, Fayard, 1965.

128   Vidalenc, J. 'L'opposition sous le Consulat et l'Empire', *Annales historiques de la Révolution française*, 1968.

129   Chiappe, J-F. *Cadoudal et la liberté*, Paris, Presses Universitaires de France, 1971.

130   Bertrand, J. *Bonaparte et le Duc D'Enghien*, Paris, Colin, 1972.

131   Lewis, G. *The Second Vendée*, Oxford University Press, 1978. On Catholic royalism in the department of the Gard.

132   Vallée, G. *La conscription dans le département de la Charente 1797–1807*, Paris, Presses Universitaires de France, 1973.

133   Vidalenc, J. 'La désertion dans le Calvados sous le premier Empire', *Revue d'histoire moderne*, 1979.

For education see the special number of *Annales historiques de la Révolution française*, 243, 1981, and:

134   Aulard, A. *Napoléon Ier et le monopole universitaire*, Paris, Plon, 1911.

135   Ponteil, F. *Histoire de l'enseignement*, Paris, Presses Universitaires de France, 1966.

136   Gontard, M. *L'enseignement primaire en France de la Révolution à la loi Guizot 1789–1833*, Paris, Les Belles Lettres, 1959.

On the social foundations of the regime, see **52** above, Ch. 3, and **38** above, Pt iii, Ch. 2, and:

137   Tulard, J. 'Problèmes sociaux de la France impériale', *Revue d'histoire moderne et contemporaine*, 1970.

138   Tulard, J. 'Les composants d'une fortune: le cas de la noblesse d'Empire', *Revue historique*, 1975.

139   Tulard, J. *La vie quotidienne des Français sous Napoléon*, Paris, Hachette, 1978.

140   Garaud, M. *La Révolution et la propriété foncière*, Paris, Presses Universitaires de France, 1960.

141   Chaussinaud-Nogaret, G., Bergeron, L. et Forster, R. 'Les notables du grand Empire en 1810', *Annales*, 1971.

142   Bergeron, L. *Banquiers, négociants et manufacturiers parisiens du Directoire à l'Empire*, 2 vols, Paris, H, Champion, 1975.

143   Boussier, A-M et Soboul, A. 'La grande propriété foncière à l'époque napoléonienne', *Annales historiques de la Révolution française*, 245, 1981.

On the economy, see above, **52**, Ch. 7; **38**, Pt iv, Ch. 6; **142** and:

144   Bergeron, L. 'Problèmes économiques de la France napoléonienne', in **106** above.

145 Crouzet, F. 'Wars, Blockade and Economic Change in Europe 1792–1815', *Journal of Economic History*, 1964.
146 Bouvier, J. 'A propos de la crise de 1805', *Revue d'histoire moderne*, 1970.

For the renewal of war in 1803 and the British war effort, see:
147 Christie, I. R. *Wars and Revolutions*, Edward Arnold, 1982, Ch. 11.
148 Emsley, C. *British Society and the French Wars*, Macmillan, 1979.
149 Glover, R. *Britain at Bay 1803–14*, Allen and Unwin, 1973.
150 Sherwig, J. M. *Guineas and Gunpowder: British foreign aid in the war with France 1793–1815*, Cambridge, Mass., Harvard University Press, 1969.
151 Howarth, D. *Trafalgar*, Fontana, 1971.
152 Lewis, M. *The Navy of Britain*, Allen and Unwin, 1948.
153 Lloyd, C. 'Navies', in **4** above.

For Napoleon's campaigns against Austria and Prussia, see **67** above, and:
154 Duffy, C. *Austerlitz*, Hampden, Conn., Archon Books, 1977.
155 Macartney, C. A. *The Habsburg Empire 1790–1918*, Weidenfeld and Nicholson, 1968, Ch. 4.
156 Falk, M. A. 'Stadion: adversaire de Napoléon 1806–1809', *Annales historiques de la Révolution française*, 1962.
157 Rothenburg, G. E. 'The Austrian Army in the Age of Metternich', *Journal of Modern History*, xl, 1968.
158 Rothenburg, G. E. *Napoleon's Great Adversaries: The Archduke Charles and the Austrian Army 1792–1814*, Batsford, 1983.
159 Langsam, W. C. *The Napoleonic Wars and German Nationalism in Austria*, New York, Columbia University Press, 1930.
160 Thiry, J. *Iéna*, Paris, Berger-Levrault, 1964.

For the Napoleonic empire, see **41–47** and **53**, above, and:
161 Connelly, O. *Napoleon's Satellite Kingdoms*, New York, Macmillan, 1965.
162 Tulard, J. *Napoléon et la noblesse d'Empire*, Paris, Tallendier, 1979.
163 Bergeron, L. et Chaussinaud-Nogaret, G. *Les Masses de Granit: cent mille notables du premier Empire*, Paris, École des Hautes Etudes, 1979.
164 Berce, Y. M. 'Société et police dans l'Ombrie napoléo-

nienne', *Annales historiques de la Révolution française*, 220, 1975.
165 Fillippini, J-P. 'Livourne sous le premier Empire', *Ibid.*
166 Kossman, E. H. *The Low Countries 1780–1940*, Oxford University Press, 1978, Chs 1–3.
167 Garnier, J-P, *Murat*, Paris, Perrin, 1959.

For the Continental System, see **144** and **145** above, and:
168 Crouzet, F. *L'économie britannique et le blocus continental 1806–1813*, 2 vols, Paris, Presses Universitaires de France, 1958.
169 Ellis, G. *Napoleon's Continental Blockade: the case of Alsace*, Oxford University Press, 1981.
170 Anderson, M. S. 'The Continental System and Russo-British relations during the Napoleonic Wars', in Bourne, K. and Watt, D. C. (eds) *Studies in International History*, Longman, 1967.
171 Hecksher, E. F. *The Continental System*, English ed., Oxford University Press, 1922.
172 Holland Rose, J. 'Napoleon and British Commerce', *English Historical Review*, 8, 1893.
173 Dufraisse, R. 'Régime douanier, blocus, système continental', *Revue d'histoire économique et sociale*, 1966.
174 Gabillard, J. 'Le financement des guerres napoléoniennes', *Revue économique*, 1953.

For Spain and the Peninsular War, see:
175 Carr, R. *Spain 1808–1939*, Oxford University Press, 1966.
176 Williams, G. A. *Goya and the Impossible Revolution*, Allen Lane, 1976.
177 Lovett, G. H. *Napoleon and the Birth of Modern Spain*, 2 vols, New York University Press, 1965.
178 Herr, R. 'God, Evil and Spain's Rising against Napoleon', in Herr, R. and Parker, H. T. (eds) *Ideas in History*, New York, Columbia University Press, 1965.
179 Sarrailh, M. 'La crise spirituelle et économique de l'Espagne à la fin du 18e siècle', *Journal of Modern History*, 27, 1955.
180 Glover, M. *The Peninsular War 1807–14*, David and Charles, 1974.
181 Glover, M. *Wellington as Military Commander*, Batsford, 1968.
182 Hibbert, C. *Corunna*, Batsford, 1961.
183 Thompson, W. F. K. (ed.) *An Ensign in the Peninsular War*, Michael Joseph, 1981.

For the Russian Campaign of 1812, see:
184   Tarlé, E. *Napoleon's Invasion of Russia 1812*, English ed. Allen and Unwin, 1942; Octagon Books, 1970.
185   Palmer, A. W. *Napoleon in Russia*, André Deutsch, 1967.
186   Palmer, A. W. *Alexander I: Tsar of War and Peace*, Weidenfeld and Nicholson, 1974.
187   Josselin, M. and D. *The Commander: Barclay de Tolly*, Oxford University Press, 1980.
188   Thiry, J. *La campagne de Russie*, Paris, Berger-Levrault, 1969.
189   Niven, A. C. *Napoleon and Alexander I*, New York, University Press of America, 1978.
190   Holmes, E. R. *Borodino 1812*, Batsford, 1971.
191   Brett-James, A. *1812: Eyewitness Accounts of Napoleon's Defeat in Russia*, Macmillan, 1966.
192   Uxkull, Baron B. *Arms and the Woman*, Secker and Warburg, 1966. A fascinating diary of the Russian campaign.

For the growth of nationalism and the revival of Prussia, see **53** above, Pt iv, and:
193   Soboul, A. (ed.) *Patriotisme et nationalisme en Europe*, Paris, Société des Etudes Robespierristes, 1973; especially Scheel's essay on Germany and Vicar's on Spain.
194   Kohn, H. 'Napoleon and the Age of Nationalism', *Journal of Modern History*, 22, 1950.
195   Simon, W. M. 'Variations in Nationalism during the Great Reform period in Prussia', *American Historical Review*, 58, 1954.
196   Meinecke, Friedrich, *The Age of German Liberation 1795–1815* (1905), Berkeley, California University Press, 1977.
197   Koch, H. W. *A History of Prussia*, Longman, 1978.
198   Shanahan, W. O. *Prussian Military Reforms 1786–1813*, New York, Columbia University Press, 1945.
199   Simon, W. M. *The Failure of the Prussian Reform Movement*, Ithaca, N. Y., Cornell University Press, 1955.
200   Craig, G. A. *The Politics of the Prussian Army*, New York, Oxford University Press, 1955.
201   Paret, P. *Yorck and the Era of Prussian Reform 1807–15*, Princeton N. J., Princeton University Press, 1966.
202   Schmitt, H. A. '1812: Stein, Alexander and the crusade against Napoleon', *Journal of Modern History*, 31, 1959.
203   Dorpalen, A. 'The German Struggle Against Napoleon: the East German View', *Journal of Modern History*, 49, 1969.

204 Parkinson, R. *The Hussar General: Blücher*, Peter Davies, 1975.

For the downfall of the Empire, see **147** above, and:
205 Palmer, A. *Metternich*, Weidenfeld and Nicholson, 1972.
206 Kissinger, H. A. *A World Restored: Metternich, Castlereagh and the Problems of Peace 1812–22*, Gollancz, 1973.
207 Kann, R. A. 'Metternich: a reappraisal of his impact on international relations', *Journal of Modern History*, 32, 1960.
208 Webster, C. K. *The Foreign Policy of Castlereagh 1812–1815*, G. Bell, 1931.
209 Hinde, W. *Castlereagh*, Collins, 1981.
210 Mackenzie, N. *The Escape from Elba*, Oxford University Press, 1982.
211 Brett-James, A. *The Hundred Days*, Macmillan, 1964. An anthology of contemporary accounts.
212 Howarth, D. *Waterloo: Day of Battle*, Fontana, 1972.
213 Keegan, J. *The Face of Battle*, Cape, 1976; Ch. 3 on Waterloo. Already a classic.
214 Cubberley, R. E. *The Role of Fouché during the Hundred Days*, Madison, Wis., Wisconsin University Press, 1969.
215 Thornton, M. J. *Napoleon After Waterloo*, Stanford, Calif., Stanford University Press, 1968.
216 Dakin, D. 'The Congress of Vienna and its antecedents' in Sked, A. (ed.) *Europe's Balance of Power*, Macmillan, 1979.

For the Napoleonic legend, see **15**, **110** and **111** above, and:
217 Dunan, M. (ed.) *Le mémorial de Saint-Hélène, par Comte de las Cases*, 2 vols, Paris, Flammarion, 1951.
218 Fleuriot, P. (ed.) *Napoleon at St Helena: Memoirs of General Bertrand*, Cassell, 1953.
219 Brookner, A. *Jacques-Louis David*, Chatto and Windus, 1981.
220 Geyl, P. *Napoleon: For and Against*, Cape, 1949.
221 Lucas-Dubreton, J. *Le Culte de Napoléon 1815–48*, Paris, Albin Michel, 1960.
222 Tulard, J. *Le Mythe de Napoléon*, Paris, Armand Colin, 1971. Edited documentary extracts.
223 Chateaubriand, F-R de *The Memoirs of Chateaubriand*, English ed., Penguin, 1965.
224 Zeldin, T. *France 1848–1945*, Vol. i, Ch 18, Oxford University Press, 1973.

Chronological Summary

1769   15 August, Napoleon born at Ajaccio, Corsica
1779   April, Military Academy at Brienne, Champagne
1784   October, *École Militaire*, Paris
1785   September, commissioned lieutenant of artillery
1786   Helped to put down workers' revolt in Lyon; to Corsica for
         nineteen months
1788   June, rejoined regiment at Auxonne
1789   September, to Corsica
1791   February, rejoined regiment in France
         October, returned to Corsica
1792   June, in Paris
         10 August, witnessed attack on Tuileries
1793   March–April, in Corsica; fled to Provence; wrote
         pro-Jacobin pamphlet
         September, given command of artillery at siege of Toulon
1794   July, execution of Robespierre; arrest and brief
         imprisonment of Bonaparte
1795   October, assisted Barras in suppressing Royalist rising
         in Paris
1796   February, given command of Army of Italy
         March, married Josephine de Beauharnais
         May, victory at Lodi, entered Milan
         August, victory at Castiglione
         October, victory at Arcola
1797   January, victory at Rivoli
         February, took Mantua
         April, armistice with Austrians at Leoben
         October, Peace of Campo Formio
1798   May, expedition sailed for Egypt
         July, Battle of the Pyramids
         August, French fleet destroyed by Nelson at Aboukir Bay
1799   February, siege of Acre in Syria
         July, defeated Turkish army at Aboukir
         August, left Egypt and his army

1799   October, landed at Fréjus
       9–10 November, *coup d'état* of Brumaire
       December, Constitution of Year VIII
1800   February, creation of the Bank of France
       June, battle of Marengo
       December, Moreau's victory over the Austrians at
         Hohenlinden
1801   February, Peace of Lunéville
       July, Concordat with the Pope
1802   March, Peace of Amiens with Britain
       August, Napoleon confirmed by plebiscite as Consul for life
1803   May, renewal of war with England
       December, invasion force assembled at Boulogne
1804   March, kidnap and execution of the Duc D'Enghien
       May, Senate proclaimed Napoleon Emperor of the French
       December, coronation in Notre Dame
1805   May, Napoleon crowned King of Italy in Milan
       August, invaded Germany
       October, French vitory at Ulm, Nelson's victory at Trafalgar
       December, battle of Austerlitz, Peace of Pressburg
1806   July, creation of the Confederation of the Rhine
       October, battles of Jena and Auerstädt
       November, Berlin Decree establishing Continental System
1807   February, battle of Eylau
       June, battle of Friedland
       July, Treaty of Tilsit; Grand Duchy of Warsaw established
       November, Junot occupied Lisbon
       December, Milan Decree extending Continental System
1808   2 May, rising against French in Madrid
       10 May, Charles IV and Ferdinand ceded their rights over
         Spain to Napoleon
       July, Joseph Bonaparte entered Madrid as King of Spain;
         defeat of a French army at Bailen
       September, Congress of Erfurt
       November, Napoleon entered Spain and recaptured Madrid
1809   Austria joined Britain in war against France
       April, battle of Eckmühl
       May, battle of Aspern-Essling
       July, battle of Wagram
       October, Peace of Vienna
       December, divorce of Napoleon and Josephine

1810 April, marriage of Napoleon and Marie-Louise
      July, Napoleon annexed Holland to France
      December, Napoleon annexed North German coast
1811 Wellesley (later Wellington) drove Masséna out of Portugal
      March, birth of the King of Rome
1812 June, crossing of the Niemen and opening of the Russian
          campaign; British and Spanish victories over the French
          in Spain.
      September, battle of Borodino; French entered Moscow
      October, French commenced retreat from Moscow; Malet
          conspiracy in Paris
      December, survivors of the *Grande Armée* re-crossed the
          Niemen
1813 February, Prussian treaty with Russia
      May, French victories at Lützen and Bautzen
      June, Wellington's victory at Vitoria
      October, battle of Leipzig; Napoleon forced to withdraw to
          the Rhine
      December, allied invasion of France
1814 February, Napoleon's initial victories
      March, fall of Paris to allies
      April, Napoleon abdicated
      May, Napoleon exiled to Elba
1815 March, Napoleon landed in France, beginning of the
          'Hundred Days'
      April, established a new parliamentary regime in France
      June, battles of Ligny, Quatre Bras, Waterloo; Napoleon's
          second abdication
      October, landed on St Helena
1821 5 May, Napoleon's death
1840 December, Napoleon's remains buried at *Les Invalides*
          in Paris
1940 Remains of the King of Rome moved from Vienna to
          Les Invalides

Index

Index

Mamelukes, 14
Mantua, 22, 45, 53
Marengo, battle of, 21, 47, 94, 101–2
Marie Louise, 63–4, 111–12, 118
Marmont, Marshal, 21, 47, 59, 70
Marseilles, 38, 39
Masséna, Marshal, 9, 20, 46, 59, 111–12
mayors, 18
Meinecke, Friedrich, 71
Mélas, General, 20
Metternich, 63, 81, 87, 88, 89
Milan, 11, 20, 46
Milan Decrees, 53
Moncy, Marshal, 85
Montebello, battle of, 21
Montesquieu, 2
Moore, Sir John, 58
Moreau, General, 11, 12, 17, 20, 21
    31, 95
Moscow, 25, 76, 77, 78
Murat, Marshal, 26, 41, 48, 49, 57, 65,
    67, 68, 69, 79, 80, 84, 88
Musset, Alfred de, 92

Naples, 11, 16, 22, 45, 46, 65, 67,
    68–9, 105–6
nationalism, 71, 72, 115–16
navy, French, 13, 14, 45–6
navy, British, 14, 45–6, 52, 58
Nelson, Admiral, 14, 22, 45
Ney, Marshal, 41, 50, 58, 80, 85, 88, 89
nobility, 41
Novi, battle of, 16

Oldenburg, Duchy of, 53, 74
opposition, 42–3

Papacy, 11, 30–1, 32, 36
Paris, 2, 3, 11, 13, 17, 18, 27, 33, 44,
    47, 65, 67, 79
Paris, first Treaty of, 86, 87, 88
Paul, Tsar, 22
Pitt, William, 22
plebiscites, 18, 23, 42, 88
Poland, 7, 50–1, 53, 74, 87–8
police, 28, 42, 71, 103–5
Pope Pius VII, 29, 30, 36, 63
population, 5–6
Portugal, 22, 51, 52, 53, 56, 57, 58, 65
prefects, 18, 32–3, 40–1

press, 27, 98–9
propaganda, 8, 32, 48, 99, 101, 103
Prussia, 6, 8, 22, 47–9, 50–1, 61, 62,
    71–3, 74, 75, 81–6, 87–8, 112
Pultusk, battle of, 50
Pyramids, battle of, 14, 101

Republicans, 31, 64
Rivoli, battle of, 11
Robespierre, Augustin, 3
Robespierre, Maximilien, 3, 4, 19, 28
Rome, King of, 63, 68, 79, 85, 90
Rousseau, 2, 27
royalists, 17, 28, 29, 31, 43, 79, 92
Russia, 7, 8, 16, 22, 46, 47, 50–1,
    52, 53, 55, 65, 68, 74–80, 81–6, 94,
    113–14

Saint Helena, 88, 90
Salamanca, battle of, 59, 77
Saliceti, 4
sans culottes, 3, 42, 100
Savary, 79, 84
Saxony, 49, 65, 87–8
Scharnhorst, 72
Schlegel, 72
Schönbrunn, Peace of, 63
Schwarzenberg, 81, 83, 84, 85
Senate, 18, 27, 40, 85, 90
Sièyes, 17, 18
Smolensk, 75, 76, 77, 78
Smith, Sir Sidney, 15
Soboul, Prof. Albert, 23
Soult, Marshal, 47, 58, 70
Spain, 9, 53, 55, 56–60, 61, 67, 68, 70,
    75, 82, 83, 84, 91–2, 94, 112, 113
Speranski, 75
Staël, Madame de, 29, 91
Stein, 72, 81
Stendhal, 92
Suvorov, General, 16
Sweden, 22, 51, 52, 53, 75
Switzerland, 20, 45, 65, 86
Syria, 13–14

tactics, 6, 8, 72–3
Talleyrand, 13, 19, 85, 88, 89
Tarlé, Prof. Eugène (Yevgeny), 77
Tilsit, Treaty of, 51–2, 74
Trafalgar, battle of, 46